score
to
soar

moving
teachers
from
evaluation
to
professional
growth

JOHN F. ELLER & SHEILA A. ELLER

Solution Tree | Press

a division of

Solution Tree

555 North Morton Street
Bloomington, IN 47404
800.733.6786 (toll free) / 812.336.7700
FAX: 812.336.7790
email: info@solution-tree.com
solution-tree.com

Visit **go.solution-tree.com/leadership** to download the reproducibles in this book.

Printed in the United States of America

19   18   17   16   15   2   3   4   5

Library of Congress Cataloging-in-Publication Data

Eller, John, 1957-
  Score to soar : moving teachers from evaluation to professional growth / John F. Eller and Sheila A. Eller.
      pages cm
  Includes bibliographical references and index.
  ISBN 978-1-936763-44-3 (perfect bound) 1. Teachers--Rating of. 2. Teachers--In-service training. 3. Follow-up in teacher training. 4. Peer review. 5. Mentoring in education. 6. School supervision. I. Eller, Sheila. II. Title.
  LB2838.E55 2015
  371.144--dc23
                                    2014050075

Solution Tree
Jeffrey C. Jones, CEO
Edmund M. Ackerman, President

Solution Tree Press
President: Douglas M. Rife
Associate Acquisitions Editor: Kari Gillesse
Editorial Director: Lesley Bolton
Managing Production Editor: Caroline Weiss
Production Editor: Tara Perkins
Copy Editors: Ashante K. Thomas and Rachel Rosolina
Proofreader: Jessi Finn
Cover Designer: Laura Kagemann
Text Designer: Rian Anderson
Compositor: Abigail Bowen

Acknowledgments

Thank you to Angie Peschel, director of curriculum and instruction, and Rob Reetz, instructional support for curriculum and instruction, from the Mounds View Public Schools for their contributions to chapter 4, "Using PLC Information."

Solution Tree Press would like to thank the following reviewers:

Dan Bechtold
Assistant Principal
Radnor High School
Wayne, Pennsylvania

David Bryant
Principal
Oak Ridge High School
Oak Ridge, Tennessee

Marguerite Dimgba
Director, Professional Learning
    Center
Greece Central School District
Rochester, New York

Russell Dyer
Principal
Collierville High School
Collierville, Tennessee

Bobbie Jo Monahan
Instructor and Principal Program
    Coordinator/Advisor
Bayh College of Education
Indiana State University
Terre Haute, Indiana

Karen Owen
Director of Professional Development
Escambia County School District
Pensacola, Florida

Michael J. Roberto
Principal
Aurora High School
Aurora, Ohio

Victoria Robinson
Professor of Educational Leadership
University of Northern Iowa
Cedar Falls, Iowa

Visit **go.solution-tree.com/leadership** to download the reproducibles in this book.

Table of Contents

About the Authors

John F. Eller, PhD, is a dynamic presenter and consultant helping educators grow and improve. He has served as an assistant superintendent, a principal in several schools, and a secondary school and elementary school teacher. John has also served as the director of the National Capital Region's Principal Preparation Program for Virginia Polytechnic Institute and State University, the executive director of the Minnesota state affiliate of the Association for Supervision and Curriculum Development, and the director of the Southwest Iowa Principals' Academy. John was honored as the Iowa Elementary Principal of the Year and a National Distinguished Principal in 1994, and one of his schools was honored as a FINE (First in the Nation in Education) school by the state of Iowa. John is currently the director of the doctoral program in Educational Administration and Leadership at St. Cloud State University, one of two public university programs in Minnesota offering an applied doctoral degree.

John specializes in teacher evaluation; leadership development; peer coaching; management of difficult people; professional learning communities; employee evaluation; conferencing skills; coaching skills; strategic planning; school improvement planning and implementation; differentiated instruction; leadership for differentiation; employee recruitment, selection, and induction; supervisory skills; and effective teaching strategies.

John has a doctorate in educational leadership and policy studies from Loyola University Chicago and a master's degree in educational leadership from the University of Nebraska at Omaha. He is the author of *Effective Group*

Facilitation in Education: How to Energize Meetings and Manage Difficult Groups and coauthor of *Working With Difficult and Resistant Staff*, *So Now You're the Superintendent!*, *Creative Strategies to Transform School Culture*, *Working With and Evaluating Difficult School Employees*, and the best-selling *Energizing Staff Meetings*.

Sheila A. Eller, EdD, has had experience in almost every education level during her leadership and teaching career. She is currently a middle school principal in the Mounds View Public Schools in Minnesota and has served as a principal in the Fairfax County Public Schools in Virginia as well as in schools in Minnesota and Illinois. She has also served as a university professor, a special education teacher, a Title I mathematics teacher, and a self-contained classroom teacher in grades 1–4.

In addition to her work in schools, Sheila has served in education on a regional and national basis. She has been a member of the executive board of the Minnesota Association for Supervision and Curriculum Development and has been a regional president of the Minnesota Elementary School Principals' Association. Sheila has a doctorate in educational administration and leadership from St. Cloud State University and holds a master's degree from Creighton University and a bachelor's degree from Iowa State University.

Sheila supports schools through her work in the areas of teacher evaluation, working with difficult and resistant staff, school turnaround and transformation, climate and culture building, effective teaching strategies, energizing staff meetings, school improvement, and other important educational topics to build effective schools. She is a regular presenter at national and regional conferences, providing practical and proven strategies for success. As an assistant professor at National-Louis University in Evanston, Illinois, she helped develop a classroom mathematics series that was adopted by several districts in the region. A video that accompanied the series featured some of her instructional techniques. Sheila has coauthored *Working With Difficult and Resistant Staff*, *Creative Strategies to Transform School Culture*, *Working With and Evaluating Difficult School Employees*, and the best-selling *Energizing Staff Meetings*.

To learn more about John and Sheila's work, visit www.ellerandassociates .com, or follow them on Twitter @jellerthree. To book John or Sheila for professional development, contact pd@solution-tree.com.

Introduction

Supervision and teacher evaluation are topics at the forefront of U.S. education and leadership. Between 2010 and 2012, at least thirty-six states made some form of policy change to their teacher evaluation processes (National Council on Teacher Quality, 2012). These changes range from simply mandating yearly evaluations of all teachers to major changes in the ways teaching is measured. Some states have changed the criteria used to evaluate teachers, while others have increased expectations for principals to identify and deal with marginal and deficient teachers.

The increased focus on teacher evaluation comes at a time when principals are already dealing with a variety of other pressures, such as budget challenges, increased calls for accountability, mandates to improve student achievement and prepare students to enter new and increasingly demanding workplaces, demands from the public for more accountability for increased educational spending, and other factors. Principals will need to find ways to work with their teachers and develop their skills while also serving as evaluators. To that effect, this book has been designed for principals, department chairs, assistant principals, superintendents, teacher leaders, charter school directors, central office administrators, and others who have an interest in helping teachers learn and grow. For simplification purposes, we will refer to all of these (and other roles charged with helping teachers grow) as supervisors, since the term encompasses the dual roles of evaluation and professional growth.

Since the early 1980s, we have seen a variety of techniques and strategies suggested for measuring teachers' effectiveness and helping them grow professionally. While many of these strategies are based on sound research, some are presented as isolated, stand-alone techniques. Supervisors may learn one or two of them, but in order to gain a comprehensive set of skills, these supervisors would have to attend countless workshops, read many books, and interact with various colleagues. For example, in some seminars, supervisors are taught that they should only coach their teachers. In other workshops, supervisors might learn how to manage the documentation required to build a case for contract termination. Because of the isolated nature of these models, it has become hard for supervisors to get an overview of multiple techniques in one location. This book serves that purpose.

The title, *Score to Soar*, was selected to highlight the changing requirements of supervisors' work with teachers to improve instruction and school effectiveness. Supervisors must find ways to not only rate their teachers on their teaching and learning practices but also use the information gathered in the supervision process to help their teachers become more effective. Similar to testing students without providing interventions to help them improve, rating teachers without facilitating their growth does nothing to improve their performance. In this book, we provide ideas that supervisors can use to go beyond simply measuring teacher effectiveness to actually increasing their effectiveness!

In some instances, only the teachers who are struggling receive attention from their principals. Helping all teachers meet minimum expectations is an important responsibility of supervisors, but there are teachers meeting this requirement who could benefit from support and encouragement to make their teaching even more effective. Without this encouragement and support, these teachers may stagnate, feel complacent, and even become disenchanted with the profession. Thus, *Score to Soar* provides supervisors with ideas and strategies to help all teachers grow, not just those who are not meeting the minimum standards.

One might think that supervisors in positions of authority directing teachers to make changes would be a successful way to ensure that professional improvement occurs. But telling people what to do does not always produce the kind of results we are looking for. Most of the strategies outlined in this book do not depend on simply giving teachers directives or telling them what to do. Instead, they are focused on clearly understanding the performance expectations and then explaining these expectations to teachers, providing the rationale for the use of evaluation strategies, and supporting teachers' use of effective teaching and learning practices.

In essence, supervisors help their teachers grow when they provide opportunities for them to learn and try new ideas. While teachers are trying these new ideas, supervisors can help them evaluate their effectiveness, determine possible refinements to their strategies, and then fine-tune them to ensure success. Many strategies we provide in this book align with existing teacher evaluation systems, so supervisors can be more efficient in their work with teachers.

The book can be read in the order it's written, or supervisors can go to a specific chapter based on their needs or interests. Chapter 1 provides an overview of the supervision process and its typical components. Chapter 2 explores creating and following a clear framework to guide teacher evaluation. Chapter 3 discusses how to ensure peer coaching is a productive experience for teachers. Chapters 4 through 7 detail how to include several types of alternative data sources in teacher evaluation to provide a comprehensive view of teachers' performance and help teachers grow professionally. Chapter 8 describes how to conduct collaborative conferences with teachers throughout the evaluation process. Chapter 9 introduces the reader to types of marginal teachers and offers strategies for how to work with marginal and deficient teachers to improve their performance. Chapter 10 provides information necessary for pursuing the termination of a deficient teacher's contract if the teacher's performance has not improved. Chapter 11 offers supervisors information that will be helpful when delivering a final summative evaluation. Several sample templates are offered throughout the chapters and in the appendices as models to help you envision the practices we describe, and reproducibles are available online at **go.solution-tree.com /leadership** to assist you in implementing these practices.

As you read this book, you'll gain important insights and ideas to help you turn your teacher evaluation efforts into opportunities to provide teachers with the support and encouragement they need to grow professionally.

chapter 1

Understanding the Elements of a Comprehensive Teacher Evaluation and Growth Process

Elaine, the superintendent of a midsized suburban school district, was getting ready to meet with her administrative team to discuss the recent state legislation that mandated more rigorous teacher evaluation processes and standards. Elaine knew that some of her principals were doing a good job evaluating and supervising their teachers while others just seemed to be going through the motions with this important task. As she reviewed the mandates for the new legislation, Elaine noticed that many of the processes were already present in the district's existing teacher evaluation procedures. She wanted to highlight the areas that would be familiar to her principals while emphasizing the new areas of focus they would have to work on in order to be successful. She also wanted to lay out the plan to ensure staff members would be able to understand core expectations and know how they would be assessed and supported.

The dilemma Elaine faced is pretty common. As U.S. states and the federal government have increased their demands for effective teacher evaluation, many school districts have scrambled to determine how the new expectations can fit into existing structures and identify the areas where they need to design and implement new teacher evaluation strategies. It's crucial for supervisors to understand the various components and expectations of their school or district's teacher growth and evaluation process.

Chapter Focus

In this chapter, you will learn the following.

▸ Roles and responsibilities of supervisors and how these roles relate to teacher evaluation processes

5

- ▸ Essential components for an effective teacher evaluation process and how these components work together to benefit teachers, including sources of data that are available to use in the supervision of teachers
  - ▸ The types of teacher contracts
  - ▸ What contract status means for supervisors
  - ▸ Why supervisors might choose to use alternative data sources and how these data sources can positively impact teachers' professional growth

These points will help you move forward in the process of supervising teachers and challenging them to learn and grow.

Roles and Responsibilities of Supervisors

Help teachers improve ↓ *Not Just evaluate*

Even though it may seem like the emphasis on teacher evaluation is new, throughout history there have been several eras in which accountability was emphasized. In the past, those in charge of teachers (local boards of education, superintendents, and principals) have served in roles that have varied from colleagues and coaches to quality-control supervisors. What we are seeing in 21st century teacher evaluation legislation is an increased focus on the principal's ability to measure and rate teacher performance. Even though the emphasis of the current legislation appears to be focused on the evaluation part of a supervisor's job, it is also necessary to focus on developing teachers' abilities to maintain and improve their levels of effectiveness. In essence, effective supervisors serve both as quality-control agents and as growth and learning facilitators.

These two roles require different approaches and skills even though their responsibilities are closely related. For example, in order to conduct the evaluation portion of their responsibilities, supervisors need to understand the school or district's performance expectations and be able to assess their teachers, judge the effectiveness of their performance, rate their skills, and use the data to assign a performance score. In order to facilitate teacher growth and learning, supervisors must also be able to determine where teachers need to improve, explain the needed skills, coach their teachers to higher levels of effectiveness, and support them during the growth process.

In addition to attending to teachers' growth individually, supervisors are expected to assess and develop the school as a whole. In order to satisfy this responsibility, supervisors use performance data to assess the essential teaching and learning areas, prioritize the most important needs of the whole staff, and then work to provide professional development and support for all staff to learn and be able to implement effective teaching strategies.

As the person responsible for the improvement of all teachers in the school, the supervisor must take the various levels of effectiveness into consideration and try to move all teachers along the continuum toward growth. We outline some of the major duties required of supervisors in table 1.1.

Table 1.1: Summary of Supervisory Roles

Supervisory Role	Major Processes Required of the Supervisor
Evaluating, rating, or grading the performance of employees	• Understand the teaching performance standards. • Determine the level of performance of individual teachers on teaching performance standards. • Prioritize the teaching performance standards that are most important or essential based on the student learning needs within the school or district. • Determine the gap between the actual and the desired teaching performance. • Determine the likelihood that the teacher can learn the skills to close the gap between the actual and expected performance.
Gathering information to assist in the development of individual employees	• Understand the teaching performance standards. • Prioritize the teaching performance standards that are most important or essential based on the student learning needs within the school or district. • Determine the level of performance of individual teachers on teaching performance standards. • Identify the difference between the teacher's performance and the required level of performance. • Identify the skills or strategies needed in order to meet the teaching performance standards. • Identify the resources needed to help the teacher gain the skills necessary to reach the teaching performance standards.
Gathering information to assist in the development of a group of employees or the entire school	• Understand the teaching performance standards. • Prioritize the teaching performance standards that are most important or essential based on the student learning needs within the school or district. • Determine the level of performance for the entire group regarding the teaching performance standards. • Identify the difference between the group's performance and the required level of performance. • Identify the skills or strategies needed in order to help the group meet the teaching performance standards. • Identify the resources needed to help the group gain the skills necessary to reach the teaching performance standards.

Essential Components of a Teacher Evaluation System

The teacher growth and evaluation systems that we have encountered have several common elements: teaching performance standards, teacher performance data sources, feedback processes, an orientation meeting, and a planning meeting. The following sections provide more detailed explanations of each element.

Teaching Performance Standards

At the center of every teacher growth and evaluation system is a set of teaching performance standards. These expectations are sometimes referred to as the teaching framework, teaching performance standards, teaching dispositions, core expectations, core competencies, or a variety of other names. For clarity purposes, throughout this book we will refer to these expectations as the teaching performance standards.

The teaching performance standards are the expectations that have been deemed essential for teachers to meet in order to be considered effective. These teaching performance standards also provide the foundation for the formative (regular) and summative (cumulative) feedback the supervisor provides during the evaluation cycle and the basis for assessing the skill level of the teachers in order to design their professional development and improvement efforts.

While these teaching performance standards may be developed locally and aligned to state or district teaching standards (Leo & Lachlan-Haché, 2012), there are also commercially developed systems that include teaching standards as part of the product. An overview of some of the common commercial teacher evaluation systems is included in chapter 2 (page 21).

Teacher Performance Data Sources

The teacher performance data sources are used to assess the performance of teachers and provide information related to the professional development of both individual teachers and the entire staff. These data sources can include almost anything that reflects the professional duties of teachers. Some of the most commonly used data sources in the teacher growth and evaluation process include the following.

- Lesson observations
- Lesson and unit plans
- Achievement data from standardized testing
- Achievement data from formative, or common, assessments

- ▶ Student perceptions of the learning environment
- ▶ Teacher portfolios
- ▶ Teachers' work as a part of a professional learning community (PLC)
- ▶ Teacher self-assessments
- ▶ Feedback from parent-teacher conferences and relationships

The types of data sources used in the teacher growth and evaluation process depend on the duties each individual teacher is expected to perform. There are several important aspects to keep in mind when working to identify the specific data sources to use in the teacher growth and evaluation process. First, the data sources should be directly related to the teaching performance standards adopted by the school or district. For example, if a supervisor is conducting an observation and is looking for evidence of student engagement, that aspect should be present in the teaching performance standards. If a supervisor works with a teacher to examine unit plans for evidence of differentiation of instructional strategies, the importance of differentiation should be present in the teaching performance standards.

Second, supervisors should inform teachers of potential data sources that will be used in the growth and evaluation process at the beginning of the school year or the process. Sharing specifics about the data sources will minimize the chances that teachers will think the supervisor is trying to "catch" them doing something wrong. If the teacher is involved in the discussion about the data sources to be used in the growth and evaluation process, the perception will be more of a collaborative working relationship than a confrontational one.

Third, when selecting data sources to use in teacher evaluation, supervisors must consider their ability to gather and use the information from the data source. For example, it may be difficult for the supervisor to gather data on a teacher's ability to interact well with parents. The supervisor may need to rely on the teacher to gather these data and discuss them with the teacher to be able to rate or score the teacher's performance. Considering the difficulty of gathering data that reflect some teaching performance standards, it is advantageous for the supervisor to work with teachers to find ways to document their performance in areas that are otherwise difficult to assess.

Feedback Processes

In feedback processes, teachers receive formative and summative information regarding their performance as it relates to the teaching performance standards. Ongoing, or formative, feedback helps them understand how they are performing at a certain point in time. Final, or summative, feedback provides them with a grade or rating based on the analysis of multiple data points. Typically, these data are gathered during the course of the year or over a multiyear time frame.

Orientation Meeting

At the beginning of each school year, all teachers on the formal growth and evaluation cycle should be involved in an orientation meeting with the principal. We will explore the details of this meeting in more depth in chapter 2, but in general, teachers need to have an opportunity to learn about the teaching performance standards, about the observation process (whether the principal is going to announce the observations, whether walkthrough data will be used in the process, and so on), what kinds of data sources will be used in the process (portfolios, peer review information, and so on), what the timelines are for the various processes, and any other information pertinent to the general evaluation process. They should also be told of any priority areas related to the teaching performance standards, the building-level goals, and any other aspects that may influence their growth and evaluation process during the upcoming cycle.

Planning Meeting

Near the beginning of the cycle, each teacher and his or her supervisor should meet to discuss specific details related to the teacher's particular evaluation. In this meeting, the discussion could focus on specific teacher goals for the upcoming year, the types of data that will be used in the growth and evaluation process, the resources that will be available to the teacher, and any other information pertinent to the experience.

Since the teaching performance standards should be used to define professional growth expectations, select data sources, and evaluate, rate, or score performance, these teaching performance standards should be the foundation for the planning meeting. It is important for the teacher and the supervisor to have discussions about their interpretations of the teaching performance standards, the data sources each feels would allow the most accurate assessment, and the potential professional growth strategies that will be available to teachers as they work to improve their instruction in these standards. These standards should be the foundation of all teaching and learning activities in the building, including mentoring activities for new teachers, teacher induction programming, recruitment and selection of new teachers, and professional development opportunities offered to teachers. Figure 1.1 illustrates the relationship between aspects of the professional support teachers receive and the teaching performance standards.

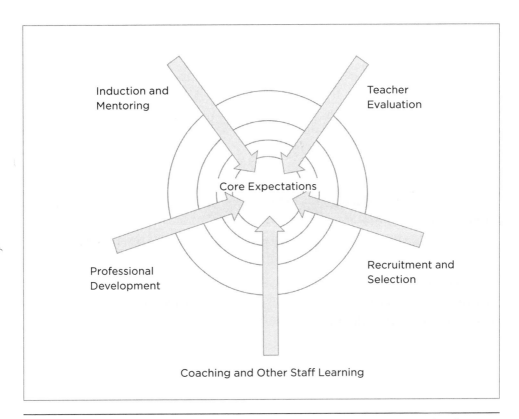

Figure 1.1: Relationships between the core expectations and other teacher growth processes.

Once a district has identified the teaching performance standards, its major teacher development processes should be based on these expectations. The alignment of these processes ensures a clear focus and growth in the essential performance areas. In theory, since all aspects of the teacher support and development program are aligned to the core performance expectations, the teachers should make continuous improvement in these essential areas.

When using the growth and evaluation process to help teachers improve, it's important to understand each individual teacher's contract status, as it may affect the way you approach his or her supervision. In the next section, we discuss contract status and its impact on the growth and evaluation process.

Types of Teacher Contracts

In many states, teachers (and other public employees) work under two distinct types of contracts—probationary and continuing. Understanding them is helpful for supervisors because slightly different strategies and techniques need to be used for each contract type. In the following sections, we'll discuss each of these. This is not designed to be a thorough legal discussion but rather an overview of the implications of the major contract types for supervisors. We encourage readers who are interested in or require more detailed or precise information to review the statutes of their particular states.

Probationary Contract (Pre-Tenure)

A teacher on a probationary contract is working on what could be described as a trial basis. During the probationary period, the teacher needs to show the supervisor his or her skills, abilities, and strengths to convince the supervisor to recommend contract renewal or extension. In many states, this period lasts from one to three years. If the teacher shows that he or she is either proficient or can become proficient in the teaching performance standards required by the school or district, the supervisor may recommend that the teacher be moved to the next contract level—the continuing contract.

Continuing Contract (Tenure)

Once a teacher has successfully completed the probationary period, that teacher may be issued a continuing contract. A continuing contract is different from a probationary contract because of the expectation of continual renewal. For example, a continuing contract is generally renewed from year to year as long as a teacher continues to meet performance expectations, follow the directives of the supervisor, exhibit good moral character, and meet other expectations as outlined in the specific state statutes related to continuing contract status. When a teacher attains continuing contract status, it is normally assumed that the teacher has successfully demonstrated competence in the teaching performance standards and the expectations of the school district. In many states, the attainment of continuing contract status means that the teacher has been deemed competent by a licensed school administrator. Once a teacher receives this designation, it becomes the burden of an administrator to prove that the teacher is no longer competent or meeting the teaching performance standards if the teacher's performance declines in the future to a point that the supervisor decides to terminate the teacher's contract. We discuss the termination process in greater depth in chapter 10 (page 155).

These conditions vary from state to state, and in several states, specific charter schools, private or parochial schools, and other unique school settings, teachers may not have access to continuing contract status. For example, in some states, charter school teachers are legally defined as at-will employees. They may not be afforded the same rights as other continuing contract teachers. We encourage you to review specific statutes or policies pertaining to contract status that apply to your school setting.

What Contract Status Means for Supervisors

From the supervisor's or employer's perspective, the probationary period is the time when the employee's skills, abilities, strengths, and performance need to be assessed and judged in relation to the teaching performance standards to determine his or her future potential. It is a time when the supervisor or employer gets to learn about the employee to determine how his or her skill set matches the needs of the school or district.

If the supervisor determines that the employee is missing needed teaching skills or strategies, he or she must decide whether these are skills that can be taught by the district using the existing professional development tools such as workshop completion, instructional coaching, mentoring, and so on. The supervisor must also determine the likelihood of the teacher being able to learn and apply these skills. If the supervisor determines that the probationary teacher has not demonstrated or cannot learn the teaching performance standards, the supervisor may recommend that the teacher's contract not be renewed. Because of the gravity of the decision to retain or dismiss a probationary teacher, it's crucial to clearly understand the teaching performance standards and to make sure teachers are assessed based on these criteria.

In most cases, when working with continuing contract teachers who face difficulties, supervisors are required to work with them to overcome the difficulties before considering contract termination. An educational administration professor we once worked with shared that "you can't fire away all of your problems." Letting a teacher go can be a traumatic and taxing process for the teacher, for the building, and for you. Obviously, the first course of action should be to help a teacher improve his or her performance and reach the standards and expectations needed to be successful in working with students.

As a supervisor, balancing all of your other duties while assessing teachers and helping them grow can be overwhelming and complex. In order to stay on top of things, you have to make teacher supervision and evaluation a part of your day-to-day duties. The integration of these roles into daily routines has been part of the drive behind the popularity of walkthrough processes and technology-based feedback systems, which allow you to capture and use informal information in the teacher evaluation process. For example, some supervisors enter their teaching performance standards into a spreadsheet using Google Drive. When they visit classrooms, they make notes on what they observe. These notes are then automatically transferred into a spreadsheet. There are many programs and applications that allow a supervisor to click on a teaching criteria section and generate a report that outlines the teacher's use of instructional strategies. Finally, districts have been able to use management tools that are web based to track teacher growth and evaluation feedback. These tools allow the supervisor to enter observational feedback and automatically generate an informational email outlining the feedback to the teacher. The supervisor can then give the teacher an option to schedule an informal conversation or reply via email with his or her thoughts about the observation.

All of these and other technology-based feedback systems still rely on the supervisor's knowledge of the teaching performance standards and ability to provide clear and accurate feedback to the teacher. Technology cannot replace the power of two people meeting to discuss the results of an observational visit or some other teaching situation, but it can do a good job in helping improve the ability to communicate more quickly and store large amounts of information. As you think about selecting technology tools to track teacher performance, keep this limitation of technology in mind.

While these observations may provide the bulk of the growth and evaluation data used to work with teachers, they may not tell the whole story of a teacher's work and performance. In addition to finding ways to informally gather data, you may also want to expand the types of data you gather.

Alternative Data Sources

Researchers Charlotte Danielson and Thomas McGreal (2000) point out that the actual lesson delivery is only a small part of what goes into teaching. According to Robert J. Marzano and Michael Toth (2013), even a supervisor who is in classrooms on a regular basis only sees a small percentage of the instruction. There are many aspects of teaching that even the most committed and dedicated observers can miss because they are not there all the time, arrive when an activity has just finished, or have to leave before an activity starts. We can get a much more comprehensive picture of the teacher's total performance by including alternative sources of data in our evaluations.

Danielson and McGreal (2000) call data sources outside the lesson observation *alternative data sources*. Figure 1.2 outlines some of the alternative data sources that could become part of the teacher assessment and evaluation process. The arch illustrates how these data sources work together to support the teacher evaluation process. Throughout this book, we will share our experiences using several of these alternative data sources. We find that many of these alternative data sources help us understand the whole picture and provide a comprehensive view of a teacher's performance.

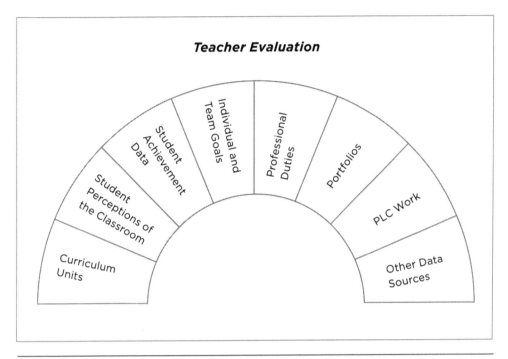

Figure 1.2: Potential alternative data sources for supervision and evaluation.

Following are explanations of each alternative data source.

▸ **Curriculum units:** Danielson and McGreal (2000) report that a majority of the interactions between teachers and students are actually focused on instructional materials, which can include textbooks, worksheets, unit packets, activities, assignments, and so on. Understanding how the teacher develops and uses instructional materials can provide supervisors with important information about the teacher's content knowledge, pacing, and instructional strategies that may be difficult to observe on a day-to-day basis.

▸ **Student perceptions of the classroom:** One of the data sources recommended by the 2012 Measures of Effective Teaching (MET) study is student surveys (Cantrell & Kane, 2013). Student feedback should be based on describing the climate and learning environment of the classroom, not focused on whether they like their teacher. Student perceptions that focus on descriptions of the classroom organization, how procedures are organized, the sense of learning opportunities present in the classroom, and other aspects that students would know and be able to describe can be very helpful in understanding life in the classroom and therefore valuable in the teacher growth and evaluation process.

▶ **Student achievement data:** The use of student achievement data is prevalent in many new teacher evaluation processes being implemented across the United States. While states are still working through the positive and negative implications of using student achievement data to assess teacher effectiveness, the fact remains that many are moving forward with using standardized and state testing information, locally developed and administered assessments, and unit and chapter tests as sources of data to evaluate teacher performance. These sources may prove helpful in understanding the teachers' impact on student growth because of their relationship to the daily work teachers do to help students learn. Also, since many of these assessments are locally developed and processed, teachers may get more meaningful and timely results that they can use to make adjustments to help students learn.

▶ **Individual and team goals:** Teachers are often involved in setting individual goals, team goals, and building goals. A teacher's work toward achieving these goals can be used as a data source to evaluate and facilitate teacher performance and growth.

▶ **Professional duties:** Teachers have professional responsibilities beyond the classroom. Some of these include working on committees, leading meetings, assuming leadership roles in professional organizations, and so on. The work teachers do as part of these extra professional duties can become good data sources for teacher evaluation and supervision. For example, a special education teacher does a certain amount of work in the classroom supporting student learning but may also spend time conducting child-study meetings, case-study evaluations, and parent-involvement sessions and working with other teachers to help them provide accommodations for special needs students. Supervisors could include some of these additional professional activities as a part of their total performance assessment to more accurately reflect a teacher's performance and responsibilities.

▶ **Portfolios:** Many teachers also have developed portfolios. Accreditation agencies like the National Board for Professional Teaching Standards require teachers to complete portfolios in order to get certified. Some states even require teachers seeking licensure and relicensure to construct portfolios that include samples of their work. Portfolios can help provide data the evaluator might not otherwise have access to. We will discuss how portfolios can be used as a part of a teacher growth and evaluation process in chapter 5 (page 83).

▶ **PLC work:** Many schools operate as PLCs to help teachers work and learn together more effectively. Supervisors can coordinate the formal teacher growth and evaluation cycle to be more in sync with the work performed in PLCs, thereby enabling the use of PLC data and the teacher's contributions to the PLC as information sources for the formal evaluation. We discuss the use of PLC data in the evaluation process in chapter 4 (page 71).

▶ **Other data sources:** As teachers and evaluators work together, there are other data sources that may emerge for use in the evaluation and supervision process. These sources could include work in leadership roles such as leading professional development workshops for other teachers (supervisors could observe one of these sessions to collect data), work with a local university providing guidance to college students aspiring to be teachers (these students could be interviewed to gain an additional data source), or any other professional practice that produces data that can be gathered and analyzed and that reflect work toward the teaching performance standards. We are limited only by our imagination and creativity.

Using these alternative data sources works best in a collaborative, collegial atmosphere where the teacher and supervisor work together to help foster continued learning and growth. Some alternative data sources are more common than others, and their use in the teacher growth and evaluation process is even mandated in several states. In chapters 4 through 7, we will explore the use of four popular alternative data sources—PLC work and goals, portfolios, student feedback, and student achievement data—in more depth. Though the use of some of these sources may not be mandated by your particular state, using these alternative data sources will provide opportunities to gain a more comprehensive understanding of the various professional accomplishments of your teachers.

A Look Back

In our example in the beginning of this chapter, Elaine was concerned about her principals and their inconsistencies in implementing teacher evaluation practices and in their understanding of the teaching performance standards. She decided that she needed to spend professional development time helping the principals develop a shared understanding and making sure core development processes such as the selection and recruitment of new teachers were aligned to these expectations.

In Elaine's district, many principals reported that they had worked with teachers to use several types of alternative data sources as a part of the evaluation process. Specifically, they had used information from curriculum planning units, parent conferences, and professional development presentations teachers had made. Elaine decided to ask the principals who had experience using these alternative data sources to talk about this process in future administrative meetings.

After spending this time concentrating on their past experiences with the teaching performance standards and alternative data sources, Elaine knew that even though they had some experience with these topics, she should provide more support and professional development for these important areas of her supervisors' work with their teachers. She knew this focus would help them get even better in their primary role of helping teachers improve and get better in their professional practice.

Chapter Summary

In this chapter, we provided an introduction to the concept of teacher evaluation and supervision and discussed the structure of teacher evaluation systems and the importance of teaching performance standards. Finally, we introduced the concept of data sources and how these sources can be used to understand the whole teacher when moving forward in the evaluation and supervision process. Alternative data sources provide evaluators, administrators, and teachers with data that are not always available or easily gathered through classroom observations. These information sources can provide a valuable, more comprehensive look into a teacher's performance. The use of alternative data sources is mandated by some state teacher evaluation processes, but even if they are not mandated by your state, you should consider their use as you work with your teachers to help them grow and learn.

As you reflect on the information you learned in this chapter, respond to the following questions.

▸ What are the specific teacher evaluation expectations in your state? What are some of the reasons for the changes to your state system?

▸ What is the purpose of the teaching performance standards and the teacher evaluation system?

▸ What are alternative data sources? How can they be used in the evaluation and supervision of teachers?

Chapter 2 will discuss the importance of understanding the teaching performance standards and expressing clear expectations for performance. The ability to convey clear expectations is a foundational skill that administrators and evaluators need in order to be effective, so in chapter 2, you'll learn strategies to help you understand and clearly articulate your expectations for teachers.

Defining Clear and Understood Performance Expectations

Dawn, an elementary school principal, was discussing her summative evaluation with Bonnie, a teacher in her building. Dawn had rated Bonnie as "developing" in the area of classroom management. When Dawn shared this rating with Bonnie, Bonnie asked, "I think I do a good job of managing my classroom. What are your thoughts, and what would I need to do in order to raise my overall score to a 'proficient' level?"

Dawn was surprised by Bonnie's questioning of her rating. As Dawn tried to answer Bonnie's question, she couldn't provide any specific information about her rating or how Bonnie could improve her summative score in the future. Bonnie left the conference with the impression that Dawn really didn't understand the evaluation criteria she was using to rate Bonnie's performance.

One of the more important and difficult aspects of using a teacher evaluation system is being able to identify and articulate the teaching performance standards and what they would look like in a classroom setting. Over the years, we have seen some principals have great difficulty with this aspect. If this foundational skill is not mastered, the rest of the process does not work well.

Chapter Focus

The ability to understand and articulate the major expectations for teachers is a crucial skill. In this chapter, you'll learn the following.

▸ Four common teacher evaluation systems designed by respected researchers

▸ Proven strategies to help you, your administrative team, and your teachers define clear performance expectations

> ▸ Methods to increase clear, detailed communication in order to articulate expectations and share examples illustrating different levels of performance

> ▸ Activities to help teachers learn and master the various teaching performance standards

> ▸ Strategies to strengthen the inter-rater reliability of supervisors assessing or evaluating the performance of teachers

Basing the evaluation process on a common set of expectations allows each teacher to know and understand the criteria for the performance evaluation.

Four Common Teacher Evaluation Systems

The teaching performance standards are best determined by the priorities, needs, and values of each district. To develop a teaching performance standards model, a district should identify its student learning needs and issues and then gather expectations outlined in research-based models that match these needs and issues. In this way, the teaching performance standards are aligned to research-based criteria and the district needs. For example, a district might have a large population of students who come to school unprepared. The performance standards for the teacher evaluation system should reflect a focus on basic learning strategies in order to help these students succeed. A school with gifted students who need a challenge should have teaching performance standards that focus on teachers' abilities to provide curriculum enrichment.

Because of time constraints and other issues, most organizations will adopt a set of teaching performance standards that has already been developed and tested. In this age of increased accountability and pressure to improve the evaluation of teachers, many teacher evaluation systems developed by researchers for large-scale use have emerged. Some of these models are being implemented on a regional basis, while others have gained popularity throughout the United States. In this section, we highlight four research-based models that have been adopted and implemented widely across the United States.

Supervisors can familiarize themselves with the following examples to gain a better understanding of their district's own needs and standards and better explain their expectations to teachers. Note that while each of these systems also contains a detailed set of evaluation processes designed to accompany the standards and focus areas, in this chapter we will only discuss the teaching performance foci for each. For more information about implementation of these evaluation systems, visit the links we provide in each section.

The Marzano Model

The Marzano Casual Teacher Evaluation Model consists of four domains spanning from classroom strategies and behavior to collegiality and professionalism. These domains include sixty detailed instructional categories for teachers and supervisors to focus on. This model is an expanded version of Robert J. Marzano's (2007) *The Art and Science of Teaching* framework. In the Marzano model, design questions are provided within several of the domain areas. These design questions give teachers an opportunity to reflect on the larger area and their efforts to impact student learning. This is a unique aspect of the Marzano model. Figure 2.1 provides an overview of the teaching performance areas within the model.

Domain 1: Classroom Strategies and Behaviors

Routine Segments

Design Question 1: What will I do to establish and communicate learning goals, track student progress, and celebrate success?

1. Providing clear learning goals and scales to measure those goals
2. Tracking student progress
3. Celebrating student success

Design Question 6: What will I do to establish and maintain classroom routines?

4. Establishing classroom routines
5. Organizing the physical layout of the classroom for learning

Content Segments

Design Question 2: What will I do to help students effectively interact with new knowledge?

1. Identifying critical information
2. Organizing students to interact with new knowledge
3. Previewing new content
4. Chunking content into "digestible bites"
5. Group processing of new information
6. Elaborating on new information
7. Recording and representing knowledge
8. Reflecting on learning

Figure 2.1: An overview of the Marzano model.   Continued →

Content Segments

Design Question 3: What will I do to help students practice and deepen their understanding of new knowledge?

9. Reviewing content
10. Organizing students to practice and deepen knowledge
11. Using homework
12. Examining similarities and differences
13. Examining errors in reasoning
14. Practicing skills, strategies, and processes
15. Revising knowledge

Design Question 4: What will I do to help students generate and test hypotheses about new knowledge?

16. Organizing students for cognitively complex tasks
17. Engaging students in cognitively complex tasks involving hypothesis generating and testing
18. Providing resources and guidance

Segments Enacted on the Spot

Design Question 5: What will I do to engage students?

1. Noticing and reacting when students are not engaged
2. Using academic games
3. Managing response rates during questioning
4. Using physical movement
5. Maintaining a lively pace
6. Demonstrating intensity and enthusiasm
7. Using friendly controversy
8. Providing opportunities for students to talk about themselves
9. Presenting unusual or intriguing information

Design Question 7: What will I do to recognize and acknowledge adherence or lack of adherence to classroom rules and procedures?

10. Demonstrating "withitness"
11. Applying consequences
12. Acknowledging adherence to rules and procedures

Segments Enacted on the Spot

Design Question 8: What will I do to establish and maintain effective relationships with students?

13. Understanding students' interests and background
14. Using behaviors that indicate affection for students
15. Displaying objectivity and control

Design Question 9: What will I do to communicate high expectations for all students?

16. Demonstrating value and respect for low-expectancy students
17. Asking questions of low-expectancy students
18. Probing incorrect answers with low-expectancy students

Domain 2: Planning and Preparing

Planning and Preparing

Planning and Preparing for Lessons and Units

1. Planning and preparing for effective scaffolding of information within lessons
2. Planning and preparing for lessons within a unit that progress toward a deep understanding and transfer of content
3. Planning and preparing for appropriate attention to established content standards

Planning and Preparing for Use of Materials and Technology

1. Planning and preparing for the use of available materials for upcoming units and lessons (e.g., manipulatives, videotapes)
2. Planning and preparing for the use of available technologies such as interactive whiteboards, response systems, and computers

Planning and Preparing for Special Needs of Students

1. Planning and preparing for the needs of English language learners
2. Planning and preparing for the needs of special education students
3. Planning and preparing for the needs of students who come from home environments that offer little support for schooling

Continued →

Domain 3: Reflecting on Teaching

Reflecting on Teaching
Evaluating Personal Performance
1. Identifying specific areas of pedagogical strength and weakness within Domain 1
2. Evaluating the effectiveness of individual lessons and units
3. Evaluating the effectiveness of specific pedagogical strategies and behaviors across different categories of students (i.e., different socioeconomic groups, different ethnic groups)
Developing and Implementing a Professional Growth Plan
1. Developing a written growth and development plan
2. Monitoring progress relative to the professional growth plan

Domain 4: Collegiality and Professionalism

Collegiality and Professionalism
Promoting a Positive Environment
1. Promoting positive interactions about colleagues
2. Promoting positive interactions about students and parents
Promoting Exchange of Ideas and Strategies
1. Seeking mentorship for areas of need or interest
2. Mentoring other teachers and sharing ideas and strategies
Promoting District and School Development
1. Adhering to district and school rules and procedures
2. Participating in district and school initiatives

Source: Marzano, Frontier, & Livingston, 2011. Used with permission.

Visit www.marzanocenter.com/teacher-evaluation for more details related to implementing the Marzano model.

The Danielson Model

Another commonly used set of teaching performance standards is found in the model developed by Charlotte Danielson. The framework has been revised several times to reflect the changing needs and dynamics of teaching and learning. Figure 2.2 provides an overview of the teaching performance areas within the Danielson model.

Domain 1: Planning and Preparation	Domain 2: Classroom Environment
1a Demonstrating Knowledge of Content and Pedagogy	2a Creating an Environment of Respect and Rapport
1b Demonstrating Knowledge of Students	2b Establishing a Culture for Learning
1c Setting Instructional Outcomes	2c Managing Classroom Procedures
1d Demonstrating Knowledge of Resources	2d Managing Student Behavior
1e Designing Coherent Instruction	2e Organizing Physical Space
1f Designing Student Assessments	
Domain 3: Instruction	**Domain 4: Professional Responsibilities**
3a Communicating With Students	4a Reflecting on Teaching
3b Using Questioning and Discussion Techniques	4b Maintaining Accurate Records
3c Engaging Students in Learning	4c Communicating With Families
3d Using Assessment in Instruction	4d Participating in a Professional Community
3e Demonstrating Flexibility and Responsiveness	4e Growing and Developing Professionally
	4f Showing Professionalism

Source: www.danielsongroup.org/framework.

Figure 2.2: The domains of the Danielson model.

The Stronge Model

A third example of a teaching performance standards model is based on the work of James Stronge (Stronge, 2015). The Stronge central framework, which delineates seven areas of teacher performance and includes several sample performance indicators for each, is highlighted in figure 2.3 (pages 28–31).

Visit www.strongeandassociates.com for more information about the Stronge evaluation system.

The Marshall Model

Another central framework many districts use is the Marshall model (Marshall, 2014), developed by Kim Marshall, a former teacher, district office administrator, and principal from the Boston area.

Performance Standard 1: Professional Knowledge

The teacher demonstrates an understanding of the curriculum, subject content, and the developmental needs of students by providing relevant learning experiences.

Sample Performance Indicators

Examples may include, but are not limited to:

The teacher—

1.1   Effectively addresses appropriate curriculum standards

1.2   Integrates key content elements and facilitates students' use of higher level thinking skills in instruction

1.3   Demonstrates an ability to link present content with past and future learning experiences, other subject areas, and real world experiences and applications

1.4   Demonstrates an accurate knowledge of the subject matter

1.5   Demonstrates skills relevant to the subject areas taught

1.6   Bases instruction on goals that reflect high expectations and an understanding of the subject

1.7   Demonstrates an understanding of the intellectual, social, emotional, and physical development of the age group

1.8   Communicates clearly and checks for understanding

Performance Standard 2: Instructional Planning

The teacher plans using the state's standards, the school's curriculum, effective strategies, resources, and data to meet the needs of all students.

Sample Performance Indicators

Examples may include, but are not limited to:

The teacher—

2.1   Uses student learning data to guide planning

2.2   Plans time realistically for pacing, content mastery, and transitions

2.3   Plans for differentiated instruction

2.4   Aligns lesson objectives to the school's curriculum and student learning needs

2.5   Develops appropriate long- and short-range plans, and adapts plans when needed

Performance Standard 3: Instructional Delivery

The teacher effectively engages students in learning by using a variety of instructional strategies in order to meet individual learning needs.

Sample Performance Indicators

Examples may include, but are not limited to:

The teacher—

3.1   Engages and maintains students in active learning

3.2   Builds upon students' existing knowledge and skills

3.3   Differentiates instruction to meet the students' needs

3.4   Reinforces learning goals consistently throughout the lesson

3.5   Uses a variety of effective instructional strategies and resources

3.6   Uses instructional technology to enhance student learning

3.7   Communicates clearly and checks for understanding

Performance Standard 4: Assessment of/for Learning

The teacher systematically gathers, analyzes, and uses all relevant data to measure student academic progress, guide instructional content and delivery methods, and provide timely feedback to both students and parents throughout the school year.

Sample Performance Indicators

Examples may include, but are not limited to:

The teacher—

4.1   Uses preassessment data to develop expectations for students, to differentiate instruction, and to document learning

4.2   Involves students in setting learning goals and monitoring their own progress

4.3   Uses a variety of assessment strategies and instruments that are valid and appropriate for the content and for the student population

4.4   Aligns student assessment with established curriculum standards and benchmarks

4.5   Uses assessment tools for both formative and summative purposes, and uses grading practices that report final mastery in relationship to content goals and objectives

4.6   Uses assessment tools for both formative and summative purposes to inform, guide, and adjust students' learning

4.7   Gives constructive and frequent feedback to students on their learning

Figure 2.3: Stronge evaluation model.

Continued →

Performance Standard 5: Learning Environment

The teacher uses resources, routines, and procedures to provide a respectful, positive, safe, student-centered environment that is conducive to learning.

Sample Performance Indicators

Examples may include, but are not limited to:

The teacher—

5.1　Arranges the classroom to maximize learning while providing a safe environment

5.2　Establishes clear expectations, with student input, for classroom rules and procedures early in the school year, and enforces them consistently and fairly

5.3　Maximizes instructional time and minimizes disruptions

5.4　Establishes a climate of trust and teamwork by being fair, caring, respectful, and enthusiastic

5.5　Promotes cultural sensitivity

5.6　Respects students' diversity, including language, culture, race, gender, and special needs

5.7　Actively listens and pays attention to students' needs and responses

5.8　Maximizes instructional learning time by working with students individually as well as in small groups or whole groups

Performance Standard 6: Professionalism

The teacher maintains a commitment to professional ethics, communicates effectively, and takes responsibility for and participates in professional growth that results in enhanced student learning.

Sample Performance Indicators

Examples may include, but are not limited to:

The teacher—

6.1　Collaborates and communicates effectively within the school community to promote students' well-being and success

6.2　Adheres to federal and state laws, school policies and ethical guidelines

6.3　Incorporates learning from professional growth opportunities into instructional practice

6.4　Sets goals for improvement of knowledge and skills

6.5　Engages in activities outside the classroom intended for school and student enhancement

6.6　Works in a collegial and collaborative manner with administrators, other school personnel, and the community

6.7　Builds positive and professional relationships with parents/guardians through frequent and effective communication concerning students' progress

6.8　Serves as a contributing member of the school's professional learning community through collaboration with teaching colleagues

6.9　Demonstrates consistent mastery of standard oral and written English in all communication

Performance Standard 7: Student Progress

The work of the teacher results in acceptable, measurable, and appropriate student academic progress.

Sample Performance Indicators

Examples may include, but are not limited to:

The teacher—

7.1　Sets acceptable, measurable and appropriate achievement goals for student academic progress based on baseline data

7.2　Documents the progress of each student throughout the year

7.3　Provides evidence that achievement goals have been met, including the state-provided growth measure when available as well as other multiple measures of student growth

7.4　Uses available performance outcome data to continually document and communicate student academic progress and develop interim learning targets

Source: Copyright to James H. Stronge. For permission to use material contact: james.stronge@strongeandassociates.com.

The Marshall model consists of criteria based on six core instructional areas:

1. Planning and preparation for learning
2. Classroom management
3. Delivery of instruction
4. Monitoring, assessment, and follow-up
5. Family and community outreach
6. Professional responsibilities

Each area has a rubric with a four-level scale (*highly effective* to *does not meet standards*) to help supervisors assess where teachers stand in all instructional areas. It's important for supervisors to base their ratings on classroom observations throughout the year rather than a single observation.

Visit http://usny.nysed.gov/rttt/teachers-leaders/practicerubrics/Docs/MarshallTeacherRubric.pdf for more information on implementation of the Marshall model.

Remember that the most effective teaching performance standards reflect the needs and priorities of the district in which they are implemented. Even if you're using a set of teaching performance standards that has been developed outside your district, you should still identify your unique needs and priorities to focus on within the framework. Visit **go.solution-tree.com /leadership** to access the reproducible "Form for Identifying Priority Teacher Evaluation Criteria" to help outline the needs and priorities in your district.

Strategies for Defining Clear Performance Expectations

It's crucial that the teachers and supervisors involved in the growth and evaluation process share a common understanding of the specific meaning and application of each criterion in the teaching performance standards. This must be addressed for the administrator to be successful in employee supervision and evaluation (Eller & Eller, 2010). Most school districts have implementation manuals for conducting the teacher growth and evaluation process. Teams of administrators and teachers who serve on committees charged with developing teacher growth and evaluation processes often create these manuals, which include details about how the process operates, the number of classroom observations that must be completed, the timelines for completion of the formative and summative feedback sessions, the various forms that have been designed to be used with the growth and evaluation process, and the teaching performance standards.

Even though the teaching performance standards and the steps and processes outlined in the manual appear to be clear and easy to understand, they may be interpreted in a different manner by other supervisors and teachers. In order to have consistent interpretation, supervisors need to talk about what they think these written standards mean, review examples of the standards, and come to a common understanding and definitions of the teaching performance standards. In the sections that follow, we present strategies that can be used in schools and districts to develop clear definitions and understandings of teaching performance standards. Some strategies are better designed for use on a districtwide basis, while others can be used in individual building-level groups, departments, collaborative teams, building leadership teams, and other school-level teams. Consider using these to help your supervisors gain a clear understanding of the teaching performance standards.

Hold Regular Discussions at Leadership and Administrative Meetings

Select an area of the teaching performance standards to focus on during an existing administrative meeting, and spend twenty to thirty minutes in small groups discussing the meaning of the criteria in that area and examples leaders would see in classrooms if teachers were meeting these core expectations. Ask each small group to present its ideas using chart paper. Give the large group an opportunity to provide feedback to each small group on the information presented, and have each small group make changes on its chart paper. At the end of the activity, collect all of the charts and transfer the contents to a Word document. These final products can be used in future leadership meeting conversations or can be organized into a booklet or manual to help leaders as they work with teachers in the future.

Ask Leaders to Provide Examples of Teaching Strategies

After discussing the meanings of the teaching performance standards descriptions, ask leaders to look for specific examples of teaching strategies as they complete their walkthroughs or other routine supervision duties that they think meet the expectations within a designated area. You may consider telling leaders to make sure their examples are so detailed, clear, and specific that their descriptions will enable others to visualize the examples as if they were standing in the classroom.

Visit **go.solution-tree.com/leadership** to access the reproducible "Form for Gathering Teaching Examples That Illustrate Successfully Meeting Performance Expectations" to assist you in the process of explaining expectations and gathering examples. Figure 2.4 (pages 34–35) provides an example of a completed form.

In figure 2.4, the classroom examples are clear and specific. This high level of clarity and specificity is something that may not come naturally to leaders. It's common for evaluators and supervisors to be general in their descriptions. You may need to push yourself or others to generate clear and specific examples to illustrate each performance area so the person reading or hearing the descriptions is able to visualize the examples.

This template is designed for you to gather specific examples of classroom strategies that help define or illustrate your teaching performance standards.

To complete the form, write a specific performance component from your teaching performance standards in the Performance Area column. Continue this process until you have filled in all rows in the column. Next, in each row in the Specific Example column, record a clear and specific example that illustrates each performance area. Finally, in the last column, explain how you think each specific example matches or illustrates the performance area.

Performance Area	Specific Example	How the Example Illustrates Successfully Meeting the Performance Area
Managing classroom procedures	In a middle school classroom, the teacher taught and had the students practice the procedures for an upcoming science lab. The teacher also had the procedures posted on the wall so all students could review them. Right before the lab, the teacher reviewed the procedures.	The teacher clearly thought through all of the steps needed in order to make the lab successful. The teacher taught and practiced the procedures, then followed up to ensure the students followed them in the lab.
Establishing a culture for learning	After providing an overview of a new science unit, the teacher described the importance of the students mastering the learning targets. After the explanation, the teacher reorganized the students into small groups and asked them to generate ideas about why it was personally important for them to master these learning targets. The small groups then reported the content of their conversations.	The teacher took one of the first steps needed to develop a culture of learning—helping the students see why the learning targets are important to them. He then asked them to generate ideas about why these learning targets are important to them.

Using instructional strategies to engage students	*A class was getting ready to provide peer feedback on a writing assignment. The teacher asked students to meet in groups of three or four in order to discuss procedures they thought would help the process work effectively. The teacher held an all-class discussion and then guided the groups to help them set guidelines for the peer feedback process. Once the guidelines were established, the teacher asked the students to meet and provide peer feedback. Every student was engaged in the discussion.*	*After establishing the procedures for conducting a peer review process, the teacher had everyone simultaneously participate in the peer review process. All students were engaged.*

Figure 2.4: Example of a completed form for gathering teaching examples that illustrate successfully meeting performance expectations.

*Visit **go.solution-tree.com/leadership** for a reproducible version of this figure.*

Methods to Increase Clear, Detailed Communication

It can be helpful for supervisors and evaluators to use different ways of thinking to help them generate more specific examples. Following are two methods of communication we have used in our professional development work with supervisors and evaluators: (1) think like a police officer and (2) think like a storyteller.

Think Like a Police Officer

When police officers document the details of a crime, they provide a step-by-step description. This description is very clear and matter-of-fact.

For example:

1. The suspect left the hotel at 7:04 a.m. in a blue, late-model pickup truck.

2. The suspect turned left on First Street and drove approximately thirty-five miles per hour to the corner of First and Vine Streets.

3. The suspect turned right on Vine Street.

For some leaders, this level of clear and precise description may be difficult to achieve, but learning to think like this will help them as they observe and write examples of teaching. It will also help them as they gather data to use in evaluating, grading, and rating the performance of their teachers. For example, if a supervisor planned to focus on how a teacher started a lesson with high levels of student engagement, the police officer description might look like this:

> At 9:05, the teacher took attendance and then asked the students, "How many of you would like to see an active volcano up close?" She waited for about thirty seconds until most of the students had raised their hands and then asked the students to stand up and find a partner. Once they had formed groups of two, she told them, "Talk in your pair groups about some of the things you might see if you were looking into an active volcano." As the students were talking in pair groups, the teacher walked around and listened in on the conversations. After about a minute of discussion, she asked three or four pairs to report what they discussed. Then the teacher asked the students to return to their seats. She said, "Today, we will learn about volcanoes, the types of active volcanoes, and how they form."

In this example, the description of the lesson is very detailed. This high level of detail will make it easier for a supervisor to see how the example fits into the teaching performance standards.

Think Like a Storyteller

Descriptions in books and novels can sometimes be so detailed that it takes several pages for an author or narrator to describe a certain setting, a situation, the clothing the main character is wearing, and so on. The extra detail these storytellers provide helps readers gain a clear understanding or picture in their minds of what's happening in the story. Authors write in such a detailed manner to make sure we have the same vision of the situation as they do.

The storyteller mindset is a good way to help supervisors achieve clarity when describing examples of teaching that meets the teaching performance standards. If a supervisor observed a teacher using appropriate pacing and structure in a lesson, the storyteller description might sound like this:

Ms. Smith started by sharing the overall objectives for the lesson and the specific learning target for the first objective. She said, "In the first part of the lesson, you will be learning about South American economies. You will be able to identify each country and the major industries that contribute to their economies." Ms. Smith first presented information about Brazil through a PowerPoint presentation and from a website about the economic aspects of Brazil. During this presentation, she had the students take notes on a note guide she had distributed to the class. This presentation took approximately ten minutes. At the end of the presentation, she handed out playing cards and asked the students to find the others in the room with the same card (the 3s looked for the 3s, the kings looked for the other kings, and so on). Once the students were reorganized into the smaller groups, she asked them to discuss what they had learned in the previous informational presentation about Brazil. The students discussed this topic for about five minutes. She got the students' attention and said, "Now, update your notes on the economic aspects of Brazil using the information you discussed in your small groups." The students took a minute to do this. Ms. Smith left the students in their small groups as she presented information on the next South American country, Argentina.

Using this high level of detail becomes helpful when the leader is completing the summative evaluation at the end of the evaluation cycle. If the supervisor has a clear vision of this performance expectation, he or she can also identify and align the proper resources to help the teacher learn and master the skills needed to be able to attain the performance level. Additionally, this method helps supervisors get into the practice of articulating detailed expectations so the teachers they supervise have a clear understanding of what is required for their teaching performance.

Activities to Learn and Master the Teaching Performance Standards

It's crucial that teachers and supervisors do more than just read about the teaching performance standards. They need to interact with these expectations in a variety of ways—visually, verbally, and kinesthetically, to name a few—to ensure understanding. We have listed some simple and straightforward activities that help educators learn and remember the teaching performance standards.

We advocate using these activities first with evaluators and supervisors since these are the people who will be leading the implementation of the teacher evaluation system. Once the evaluators and supervisors are clear about the meaning of the performance indicators, it's important that the same level of knowledge is brought to the teachers. The techniques and activities discussed here will help evaluators and administrators better understand performance expectations and will also work well at the faculty level.

Illustrative Presentations

An earlier version of this activity appears in Eller & Eller, 2006.

In this activity, we ask group members to develop a short presentation, demonstration, or skit focusing on a component or a subcategory of the teaching performance standards. The steps of the activity are as follows.

1. Divide the group into smaller teams of three to four people.

2. Assign each small team one teaching area, specification, or attribute from the teaching performance standards.

3. Ask each small team to develop a meaningful two- to three-minute presentation that will help illustrate its assigned area, specification, or attribute. Give the teams about ten minutes to develop this presentation.

4. Once all the teams have completed the planning, have them give their presentations. The remaining large-group members watch the presentation and provide each team feedback on its presentation. The large group also discusses what it learned as a result of the presentation.

Each team may develop a skit that clearly illustrates the teaching performance standard component or shows a common problem encountered with implementing the assigned component.

For example, one team developed a short skit showing the implementation of using effective questioning techniques. In this skit, it illustrated a teacher asking an entire class questions, then calling on several individuals to provide responses. The skit was fun to watch, and it illustrated good questioning techniques.

In another presentation, a small group developed a short jingle to illustrate the concept of designing and implementing assessments that match the learning targets from the school's teaching performance standards. In the jingle, the group sang about the factors that should be taken into account when developing assessments, including the proper level of difficulty, the best ways to demonstrate learning for students, ways to ensure that the assessments are reliable, and other aspects that should be taken into consideration when developing and implementing assessments. The jingle only lasted about a minute, but it received applause from the rest of the staff. It helped teachers remember the main ideas for designing and implementing assessments.

Large-group discussions at the end of each presentation are valuable because they help participants gain a better understanding of the expectations for the teaching performance standards being illustrated in these presentations.

Carouseling Activity

An earlier version of this activity appears in Eller & Eller, 2006.

In the carouseling activity, group members get an active learning opportunity to generate specific examples of the components of the teaching performance standards. Carouseling can be a fun and engaging activity that helps teachers deepen their understanding of the specific attributes of and expectations for teaching. The activity works as follows.

1. As facilitator, divide the large group into smaller groups of four to five.

2. Assign each of the smaller groups a component or teaching area from the teaching performance standards. Ask each small group to provide a clear and detailed definition of its assigned item and examples of what it would see in a classroom if the item were being implemented. The group's example should be highly detailed so that readers can visualize it being implemented. Give the groups about ten minutes to complete this first part of the activity and record their work on chart paper. As they are working to complete their tasks, walk around and help guide the small groups to ensure that they provide very detailed examples.

3. Once all the groups have completed step 2, assign new roles within the small groups. Approximately one-half of the group will be designated as *stayers*, and the other half will be designated as *travelers*. Stayers stay at their chart and explain their group's work to travelers, who visit each chart. Ask each of the small groups to designate the travelers and stayers and make sure everyone in the group understands the procedure for the activity.

4. Play music to signal the travelers to rotate clockwise from group to group and provide feedback on the definitions and examples generated by each group they visit. Travelers can write suggestions for improving clarity directly on the chart.

5. When you see that most of the groups are finishing the activity, start another song and have the travelers move to the next group.

6. The carouseling activity continues until the travelers have visited most of the charts.

Once the activity is complete, the facilitator can open up discussion with the travelers from each group about what they learned as they traveled from group to group and also ask the stayers to tell what they learned from the various travelers. Topics of discussion could be the level of specificity in the teaching examples, the clarity of the definitions of the teacher performance standards, the terms that the groups were able to clarify, and so on. Opening up the conversation to the entire group helps everyone learn and hear what others gained by participating in the activity.

Once all the charts have been refined, you can gather them up and transfer the contents to a Word document. You can then use these typed teaching examples in future meetings or develop an example guidebook for evaluators to use when describing desired teaching behaviors during conferences with staff to help them improve their performance. Providing teachers with these resources can also help them become much more engaged in their own evaluation and growth.

We have used this activity with thousands of leaders with great success. Most of those we work with comment on how important it is for them to see how others describe teaching examples and how their examples can be refined.

Rapid Articulation

In this fun and engaging activity, leaders are put into pairs and are given a limited amount of time to articulate their understanding of and priorities for the teaching performance standards. It is called *rapid articulation* because it requires both parties in the conversation to share their thoughts in a rapid manner. This is helpful to those participating in the activity because they will get several opportunities to think out loud about their understanding of some of the different components of the teaching performance standards. By talking about them several times during the activity, they will make the components a more permanent part of their memory so they are easier to recall and explain in real-life situations, raising their credibility and confidence in working with the standards.

The following outlines how the activity works.

1. Give individuals ten minutes to write a definition and two examples of teaching behaviors associated with an assigned teaching performance standard. These definitions and examples should

illustrate teaching behaviors that are at least meeting the district standards. The examples should be detailed enough that they can be easily understood when presented.

2. Once they have completed their definitions and examples, tell them to pair up with another person. Have them stand in their pairs while gathering in a configuration that includes an inner circle and an outer circle. The pair member wearing the lightest-colored shirt joins the inner circle. These light-shirted members have their backs toward the inside of the circle while they face out. The other half of the pair stands in a circle facing inward toward their light-shirted team member. See figure 2.5 for an example of this arrangement. Note that many pairs can do the activity simultaneously.

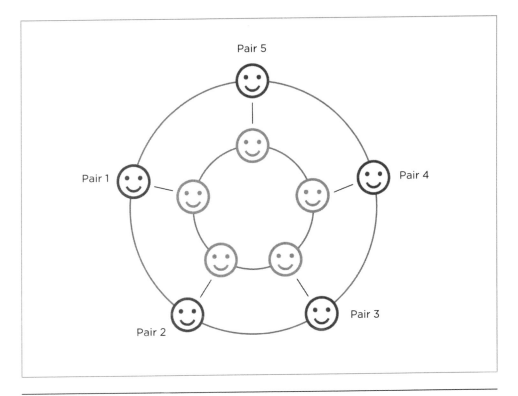

Figure 2.5: Illustration of rapid articulation pair arrangement.

3. Tell them that the pair member in the inner circle will go first and explain his or her definitions and examples. Once the inner-circle person has finished, the outer person will get an opportunity to do the same.

4. Tell the team members that when you notice the outer circle members have completed their descriptions, you'll have them rotate one person clockwise. When a song comes on, that will be the signal that the outer circle members need to move one person clockwise. When they get to their new inner-circle person, the process will be repeated. Repeat this process five to six times to give each person ample opportunities to explain his or her definitions and examples.

5. When you have completed five to six rotations, ask participants to talk in their existing pair groups about how the activity has helped them understand and articulate their definitions and examples. Have participants share what they learned as a result of the activity with the larger group.

Matrix of Expectations

Developing a matrix that provides performance descriptions and examples will be helpful. Divide participants into groups of three to four people. Each group is issued chart paper and markers and is assigned a teaching performance standard. Groups are then asked to generate one example within each of the performance ratings the district uses. Figure 2.6 illustrates an example of a blank matrix.

Performance Area:	
Not Meeting District Standards	Partially Meeting District Standards
Proficient Related to District Standards	Exceeds District Standards

Figure 2.6: Matrix of expectations.

The matrix in figure 2.6 includes four performance levels. If you choose to use this activity, your matrices can include whatever number of distinct levels or descriptors that your teacher evaluation system uses in its scoring protocol. Each matrix will only focus on one example. As a supervisor, you'll need to think about how you will eventually rate or score the teacher's overall performance. Developing these examples with teacher groups will help provide a guide for you and your teachers to understand the criteria for the different ratings. Keep in mind that the process of providing a final rating or score will depend on the combination of the quality and the consistency of the teacher's performance. We will talk more about this process in chapter 11 (page 167).

We have included a completed matrix in figure 2.7 as an example of the level of specificity you'll need from your teams in this activity.

Performance Area: Managing Classroom Expectations	
Not Meeting District Standards	**Partially Meeting District Standards**
The teacher has little or no classroom management process in place. Students are consistently off task. The teacher spends much of the class time attending to off-task behavior. The teacher deals with the same issues repeatedly.	The teacher has a basic classroom management process in place. Students are off task on a regular basis, but some order is maintained so that the basic goals of the lesson can be attained. The basic behavior issues have been addressed. The teacher is spending time dealing with complex or changing behavior problems.
Proficient Related to District Standards	**Exceeds District Standards**
The teacher has a sound classroom management process in place. Provisions are made to handle basic administrative tasks (attendance, opening activities, and so on) automatically so the teacher can concentrate on teaching and learning processes. Behavior expectations have become regular processes (habits) for students. Classroom instruction is rarely interrupted by behavior problems. If off-task behavior occurs, the teacher handles it in a discreet and positive manner.	Classroom procedures and the management plan are solidly in place. All administrative tasks (attendance, opening activities, and so on) are handled automatically with no instructional time taken for these tasks. Teacher constantly tracks and monitors student behaviors and heads off potential issues before they emerge. Students are meaningfully engaged in self-monitoring the classroom and their own behavior. A variety of learning processes and procedures have been taught and practiced so they can be implemented with minimal direction. The teacher is able to spend 100 percent of class time facilitating learning since students are able to work independently and in groups with minimal disruption.

Figure 2.7: Sample matrix of expectations.

Video Examples

Several of the evaluation methods highlighted earlier in this chapter feature videos of teachers using desired strategies in classroom settings. However, even if your district does not purchase an evaluation model that includes videos, it's possible to access similar teaching videos. Because of the implementation of the Common Core State Standards (National Governors Association Center for Best Practices & Council of Chief State School Officers, 2010), there are many websites that feature videos illustrating effective teaching practices, including Teaching Channel (www.teachingchannel.org), Khan Academy (www.khanacademy.org), and TeacherTube (www.teachertube .com). These videos can be used for training or to provide examples for teachers and administrators. Some of these videos simply show teachers working with students, while others are labeled or contain bookmarks to tell the viewer at what point in the video the desired model is illustrated.

Once the faculty and administrator have conducted conversations to clarify performance expectations, collaborative teams or other groups can be charged with finding videos that reflect the use of effective teaching strategies. These videos can be shown at faculty meetings to facilitate discussions, or the links can be posted or shared for faculty to review on their own. These videos can provide a clear picture of what the desired teaching strategies may look like, and searching for them helps build faculty understanding of the criteria for, as well as a clear picture of, effective teaching.

Feature Attributes of the Month

An effective activity to help educators focus on and learn teaching performance standards is to feature one or two standards as Attributes of the Month. For example, a school might designate November as Classroom Management month. During this month, staff members are asked to gather examples of effective classroom management. These examples are then discussed at faculty meetings, submitted to the principal, and discussed at collaborative team meetings. At some point during the month, the examples are shared with the entire faculty in writing or verbally. Once each aspect has been shared, the faculty can engage in a conversation about the example and how it matches or does not match their understanding of the standards. This helps staff identify and know the various evaluation expectations. Teachers can also discuss how they could use the examples to grow their own teaching skills.

PLC Discussions of Expectations

Many districts have become PLCs to help teachers focus on their professional learning. In a PLC, teachers can discuss teacher performance standards and examples relative to the entire school community. The specific teacher performance standards for discussion can be assigned, or collaborative teams can select their areas of focus. Periodically, these teams should report back to the larger faculty on their work in these areas. These reports should focus on presenting explanations and examples of the teacher performance standards rather than providing definitions for the exact levels of performance expected of teachers. The administration should be responsible for setting and following through on what the exact scoring levels are regarding the evaluation of these standards.

Strategies to Strengthen Inter-Rater Reliability

The MET study recommends that multiple evaluators observe teachers (Cantrell & Kane, 2013); this concept is what we refer to as *inter-rater reliability*. The information from these evaluators is then integrated in the final grading or scoring of teachers. In some buildings, there are multiple evaluators who divide up the observations to make sure that each teacher is observed by at least two different people. In settings where there is only one evaluator, an outside observer may need to assist in the observations. When multiple observers are involved, they need to work together to make sure they have a shared understanding of the criteria and provide clear and consistent feedback. We suggest the following strategies to increase inter-rater reliability.

▸ Hold ongoing discussions about the criteria and levels of performance related to the teaching performance standards. These ongoing discussions help monitor and adjust evaluator perceptions and understandings of performance criteria.

▸ Offer training in the performance criteria. When evaluators get training and support to better understand the various aspects of the performance descriptions for the teaching performance standards, they are able to give more consistent feedback and scores related to teacher performance.

▸ View videos of teaching, and talk about what was observed and why it merited a certain rating.

▸ Read and review evaluators' performance assessments and provide feedback. District office staff and other supervisors can also review the evaluators' reports and give feedback about how they score or rate their teachers and about the evidence they provide to the teachers.

While inter-rater reliability is desirable to attain within a school district, it is crucial to attain within a building. If multiple observers score the same teacher differently within a building, the teacher gets mixed messages and can become confused.

A Look Back

Earlier in this chapter, we introduced you to Dawn and Bonnie. In the example, Dawn had trouble letting Bonnie know what her expectations were for her level of performance. Dawn decided to try a new strategy to help her be more clear and detailed in her expectations. She set aside time after school (before regularly scheduled night meetings) to think about her expectations for three or four of the areas she commonly discussed with staff, and she used the police officer thought process to identify the details she would see in a classroom if the teacher was proficient and exceeded the expectations outlined by the district in those areas. She wrote down the specific step-by-step descriptions for these performance levels so she could use them in future conversations with faculty.

In a follow-up meeting with Bonnie, Dawn started by saying, "In our last meeting, you asked about my expectations regarding a proficient rating. I've given your question more thought, and I have some examples. Once I present these, let's talk about how the examples apply to you or how we might need to adjust our thoughts based on your unique situation."

Dawn presented her examples from a position of authority rather than feeling like she was on the defensive (like she did in her earlier conversation). She also left the door open for further conversations with Bonnie and got her involved in helping document data to justify the proficient rating. In the end, it was a productive conversation that helped Dawn and Bonnie connect in a collaborative manner.

In future conversations, Dawn asked Bonnie for examples of data they could use to help document Bonnie's performance. Bonnie was becoming an active participant and a true partner in the process rather than having the evaluation done to her; she was able to learn and improve her performance as a result of this partnership.

This interaction between Dawn and Bonnie shows how the supervision and evaluation process can be conducted in a collaborative manner. As evaluators and supervisors, we set the standards for performance, but we also want to engage the teachers in understanding the teaching performance standards. It's important that teachers have a meaningful role in their own supervision, because in order for them to learn, they need to be engaged. This collaboration is a key aspect of the supervision process.

Chapter Summary

In this chapter, we examined ways to structure your teacher evaluation process and suggested strategies for clearly defining and communicating expectations to teachers and ensuring consistency among evaluators. The teaching performance standards determine the criteria that will be used to measure teachers' performance and help them develop their skills. While some districts develop their own teaching performance standards, most use established and tested models. The evaluation methods provided in this chapter share common definitions, criteria, and descriptions.

Developing a clear and common understanding of all aspects of the teaching performance standards is essential for effective implementation of the evaluation and growth process. It is the responsibility of districts to take the time to ensure that evaluators, administrators, and teachers clearly understand the terms, descriptions, and performance expectations found in the teaching performance standards. Each district should customize its evaluation model to its unique set of needs.

As you reflect on the information you learned in this chapter, respond to the following questions.

▸ What are some of the critical aspects that need to be taken into account when adopting or creating a set of teaching performance standards?

▸ How can general teaching performance standards be adapted to reflect local needs and priorities?

▸ What strategies can help ensure that administrators and teachers understand the teaching performance standards?

In the next chapter, we begin our discussion of peer coaching within the teacher supervision and evaluation process. Data gathered in the peer review or peer coaching process can be great assets for not only teacher evaluation but also for the teacher's professional growth. As you read the chapter, be sure to focus on the teaching performance standards and how you could gather data that reflect these priorities.

chapter 3

Using Information From the Peer Coaching Process

Tanya, a sixth-grade teacher, had worked with her peer reviewer, Bill, to establish her professional goals for the year. One of these goals was to increase the meaningful involvement of her students as she taught lessons. Today, her peer reviewer came by to observe her students and see how they were involved in the instruction.

After the observation, Bill shared some student involvement observational data with Tanya. Rather than telling Tanya whether the strategies she used were effective, Bill decided to use coaching strategies with Tanya. He asked her how she thought the lesson and the student involvement went. She responded that she thought it went well. Bill followed up by asking Tanya what she observed that let her know the lesson was successful, and she shared some of the things she noticed. In the end, Bill asked Tanya to share what she learned in the conference and how she planned to use this learning in future lessons. Tanya shared her thoughts and thanked Bill for taking the time to work with her.

In this example, we see how Tanya and Bill work together as peers to help Tanya grow as a professional. This is an example of a process called *peer review* or *peer coaching*. We have chosen to use the term *peer coaching* throughout this book, but these terms are often used interchangeably. Both terms refer to a process in which teachers have an opportunity to set one or more professional growth goals, then work with a peer to help them reach these goals. Another aspect of the peer coaching process is that teachers have opportunities to observe each other and share their thoughts about the observations. Peer coaches are typically fellow teachers, but supervisors may also be engaged in coaching relationships with teachers. The ideas in this chapter are provided for supervisors who fulfill coaching roles, supervisors tasked with implementing a teacher growth and evaluation process that includes peer coaching, and teachers who are engaged as peer coaches.

Chapter Focus

The supervisor in charge of implementing or coordinating the teacher growth and evaluation process needs to understand how the peer coaching portion works, what kinds of processes need to be in place, and how to support teachers who are either peer coaches or being coached by peers. Peer coaches need the proper training and support to coach their colleagues. Several of the strategies presented in this book will help peer coaches assist their colleagues in setting goals, planning effective activities, and discussing events they have observed as a part of their peer coaching tasks. Supervisors who perform coaching duties must understand that coaching a teacher is a different process than evaluating a teacher. In coaching, the teacher is being assisted or guided toward growth, while in evaluation, the growth might be more prescribed or directed. The goal setting and coaching strategies provided will be helpful to supervisors who wish to implement this type of growth process with their teachers. In this chapter, readers will learn the following.

- ▸ When to use peer coaching, including descriptions of several different conferencing processes to implement

- ▸ How peer coaching is part of the teacher growth and evaluation process, and the importance of training the coaches

- ▸ Ways to include goal setting both formally and informally to push teachers to grow in specific areas, including the use of SMART goals and a pre-event coaching conference

- ▸ Coaching skills that will help coaches develop a rapport with the coachees, including listening well, learning to paraphrase and reflect, and designing good questions

When to Use Peer Coaching

In general, peer coaching involves goal setting, classroom observations, feedback, and a final review of the progress on the initial goal. Teachers can ask for specific feedback and coaching for areas of interest and areas of potential growth. Some of the occasions when peer coaching can be used include:

- Helping a teacher implement a specific set of instructional strategies
- Assisting a teacher in planning or developing a lesson, unit, project, and so on
- Assisting a teacher in developing and implementing assessments
- Problem solving in instructional situations
- Helping a teacher try out a new idea or strategy for the classroom
- Assisting a teacher who is dealing with a recurring instructional issue
- Working with a teacher to develop team teaching strategies

Typically, peer coaching will involve a conference or small-group or individual instruction on a topic, with the person or group being coached thinking through the issue. The peer coach may choose to share information with the teacher, work together with the teacher to solve a problem, or ask questions of the teacher to help him or her develop ideas or strategies to address the situation. Growth for the person or group being coached will be facilitated through several conferencing processes including:

- **A pre-event conference**—In this type of conference, the coachee is asked to think through an upcoming teaching event. Pre-event conferences are useful for setting professional growth goals, planning meetings, planning lessons and units, getting ready for parent conferences, preparing to attend professional development events, and so on. Pre-event conferences help the coachee focus his or her thoughts about the upcoming event and look toward specific outcomes and ways to measure the event's success. The peer coach can help the coachee by asking questions and sharing information and ideas.

- **A mid-event conference**—In this type of conference, the coach talks with the coachee in the middle of a teaching unit or long-term event. The coach helps the coachee learn from what has already been done and make any needed midcourse adjustments or corrections. Mid-event conferences are good for helping teachers evaluate their implementation efforts and adjust their strategies if needed.

- **A post-event conference**—This type of conference provides the coachee with an opportunity to reflect on an event once it has been completed, discuss it with the coach to gain perspective on the level of success, and self-evaluate. An event could be a lesson, unit, or meeting the teacher has conducted or a parent-teacher conference. One major purpose of a post-event conference is to help the coachee learn from the event in order to transfer this learning to similar experiences in the future.

Peer coaches or supervisors may choose to use one or all of these conference processes to help the teachers they work with expand their thinking and self-reflect on their teaching. Supervisors who support peer coaches should share this information with them so they can use it to determine what types of conferences would be best for those they coach.

Peer Coaching as a Part of the Teacher Growth and Evaluation Process

Peer review or peer coaching has been identified as a part of various state statutes and evaluation processes. In most of the state requirements, the information from the peer coaching or peer review process is collected during the "off years" of the teacher evaluation process—the years when the teacher is not under formal review.

Another aspect common among state requirements is using the peer coaching process to help the individual teacher set and work toward professional growth goals. These goals can be based on aspects of the teaching performance standards identified in the last formal review cycle with the principal, or they can be based on a professional need identified by the teacher or with the assistance of the peer coach or reviewer.

In many state teacher evaluation processes, the teacher can choose whether to share the peer coaching topics, feedback, and results with his or her supervisor. This is significant because the teacher is in control of the information. A peer coach cannot report to the supervisor or share any of the information from the peer review process. In theory, the confidentiality of the peer coaching relationship makes the process more open and honest. Since the information from the peer coaching process is confidential, teachers might be wise to explore areas needing improvement based on previous feedback from their supervisor. They could use their peer coaching partner to help them enhance their strategies so that the next time they are scheduled to be formally evaluated by their supervisor, they can be better prepared.

Peer coaching is a concept that holds great promise but also can make some teachers nervous. They may feel reluctant to evaluate or rate a peer. Some may feel that they don't have much to offer their peers as a coach or may not be excited about trying to help their colleagues change and grow. Because of these potentially negative aspects, it's a good idea to have clear guidelines in place for a peer coaching process and to provide teachers entering the peer coaching process with basic professional development opportunities about the scope of peer coaching, the skills required, strategies to deal with teacher growth and change, techniques for goal setting and helping teachers attain their goals, and providing nonjudgmental coaching and feedback as a peer coach. We will be sharing information related to these processes throughout the chapter. If peer coaching is implemented correctly, it can be a real opportunity for growth.

When tying together the aspects of peer coaching and the teacher evaluation process, schools often divide their teachers into three groups. About one-third of the teachers are formally observed by the principal, while two-thirds of the teachers are involved in the peer coaching process. Each year, a new group of teachers is under the principal's formal observation. Figure 3.1 illustrates a sample peer coaching cycle.

	Teacher Group I	Teacher Group II	Teacher Group III
Year 1	Supervisor Observation and Evaluation	Peer Coaching	Peer Coaching
Year 2	Peer Coaching	Supervisor Observation and Evaluation	Peer Coaching
Year 3	Peer Coaching	Peer Coaching	Supervisor Observation and Evaluation

Figure 3.1: Sample peer coaching cycle.

During the peer coaching years, the teacher typically works with his or her coach to set professional growth goals and get coaching and feedback on these goals. The goals should be related to the teaching performance standards. During the formal evaluation year, a supervisor observes the teacher and completes a summative evaluation document.

Goal Setting

The number of goals a teacher works on during the peer coaching years varies depending on the district, but it's important to focus on two or three goals rather than trying to set and reach a larger number of goals. The goal-setting process can range from an informal conversation between the teacher and peer coach to a more formal process involving forms, specific outcomes, and deadlines. See figure 3.2 (page 54) for a sample professional growth goal-setting form to consider when helping teachers set professional growth goals. Keep in mind that we provide this as an example, and you may want to adjust this form or develop a different tool so as to align to your evaluation system and teaching performance standards.

General Growth Goal	Specific Skills Desired or Needed to Reach Goal	Methods to Attain Skills	Timeline	What It Will Look Like When I've Completed This Goal

Source: Adapted from Eller, 2004.

Figure 3.2: Sample professional growth goal-setting form.

We designed this form to provide a concrete method to guide the goal-setting process. Here are the steps for using this form.

1. First, ask the teacher to generate one to three general goal statements. These goal statements should be written in column 1.

2. Once the teacher has listed two to three general goals, ask him or her to move to the last column (What It Will Look Like When I've Completed This Goal) and write in his or her vision for the completed goal. This is important because completing this column will help the teacher envision the completed goal and will provide the indicators of success. This is an area where coaching and allowing the teacher to set the vision for the goal helps him or her own the goal.

3. After the vision has been developed, have the teacher move to the second column (Specific Skills Desired or Needed to Reach Goal) and list some of the strategies needed to reach the goals.

4. After the specific strategies to attain the goal have been identified, ask the teacher to complete the third column (Methods to Attain Skills). In this column, the teacher lists the specific methods he or she will use to attain each of the specific skills in column 2. Adding this information will help the teacher identify the critical strategies needed to attain the skills to meet the goal.

5. Once the third column (Methods to Attain Skills) has been completed, ask the teacher to complete column 4 (Timeline). In this column, the teacher lists the timeline for each of the methods and strategies from column 3. By completing the timelines, the teacher will now have a plan in place that can be implemented over the course of the year.

Once the professional growth goal-setting form has been developed, it can be used in coaching the teacher toward the successful attainment of the goals.

Setting SMART Goals

Another method to help teachers set strong goals is to use the SMART (specific, measurable, attainable, realistic, timely) acronym to guide the process. The SMART goal process is very common and is sometimes applied to school-based or team goals. As a coach, you will want to help your coachee set and reach effective goals. As a supervisor, you'll want to assist your teachers in outlining the specifics of the SMART acronym as they set their goals. No matter what your role is in the teacher supervision process, consider the following as you work with teachers to set effective goals.

▸ **Specific:** A goal has a greater chance of being met if it is specific in nature. Consider the following six questions when designing specific goals.

1. **Who** is involved?
2. **What** is going to be accomplished?
3. **Where** will this goal take place?
4. **What** is the timeline for this goal to be accomplished?
5. **What** are the specific requirements and constraints that outline this goal?
6. **What** are the purposes for completing this goal?

▸ **Measurable:** The goal should be measurable. Set the criteria up front for what it will look like when the coachee reaches this goal. A good question people ask themselves is, "How will I know when the goal has been accomplished?"

▸ **Attainable:** The goal should provide a stretch but be within reach of the coachee. The term *stretch* refers to the fact that the goal should be based on the teacher attempting a goal or set of goals that is just beyond his or her present level of operation. This means that the teacher should not select goals related to things he or she already knows how to do or has already attained. It also means that he or she should not attempt goals that are way out of reach or impossible to attain. The stretch balances the possibility of reaching the goal with having to work in order to reach it. The goal may require intermediate steps, but it should be something of interest to and reachable for the coachee.

▸ **Realistic:** A goal needs to be realistic if it is to be accomplished. This aspect is related to the attainable component but focuses more on instilling the belief that the goal is within the scope of the job and the time and resources available to the coachee.

▸ **Timely:** A good goal must have a time frame for its attainment. This provides an outer boundary under which the goal will be worked on and accomplished.

Using a Pre-Event Coaching Conference

Another strategy to help teachers set professional growth goals is to use a pre-event coaching conference to help the teacher think through the goal-setting process. In this section, we provide several tools coaches use toward this purpose. Coaches can guide the teacher through a pre-event conference to set goals using the following steps.

1. Ask the person being coached to describe his or her general ideas about what he or she would like to accomplish during the peer coaching experience. For example:

   ▸ "What are you trying to accomplish this school year?"

   ▸ "In what areas do you want to grow as a teacher?"

   ▸ "What kinds of ideas do you have to improve your classroom this year?"

   ▸ "What are you thinking about regarding your growth as a teacher in the upcoming year?"

2. Ask the person being coached to focus on two to three specific goals he or she wants to work on in the peer coaching process. For example:

   ▸ "In relation to your general goals, what are one or two specific goals you want to work on for the upcoming year?"

   ▸ "Since it would be difficult to reach goals during this school year in all of the areas you just talked to me about, what are two specific goals you want to reach?"

- ▸ "If you had to focus this area down to just two goals, what would they be?"
- ▸ "Most people are more successful when their goals are focused. What are the two areas you really want to focus on for this school year?"

3. Ask the person being coached to list what specific activities, information, professional development, and so on that he or she needs in order to accomplish his or her professional goals. For example:

    - ▸ "Since you've identified this as a goal area, what specific strategies will you need to use to be successful?"
    - ▸ "Think about your plan for this goal. What techniques and strategies will you need to implement in order to be successful?"
    - ▸ "You've been clear about where you are going. Now let's look at some of the ideas and strategies that will help you reach your destination. What do you think would be the two most essential strategies you need to use in order to be successful?"
    - ▸ "What do you think you will need to do in order to reach this goal? List one or two strategies."

4. Ask the person being coached to share what evidence he or she will gather to assess how he or she is doing on the professional growth goals. For example:

    - ▸ "What will you need to see, hear, and feel in order to know you have reached this goal?"
    - ▸ "What will it look like when you reach this goal?"
    - ▸ "If I came to your classroom after you had reached this goal, what would I see? What would people be saying to me? How would your classroom look different than it does now?"
    - ▸ "How will you know when you are successful with the goal?"

5. Ask the person being coached to share how the coach can assist him or her in reaching his or her professional growth goals. For example:

    - ▸ "My job is to assist you in your efforts to reach your goals. How can I best serve you as a coach?"
    - ▸ "What would be helpful for you to receive from me as your coach during the year?"

▸ "As a coach, I can do a variety of things to assist you. What would you like me to do to help you?"

▸ "As your coach, what would you like me to focus on when I visit your classroom?"

Visit **go.solution-tree.com/leadership** for the blank reproducible "Goal-Setting Planning Template" that follows these steps. Feel free to adapt or change the questions to suit your specific needs.

Coaches can use the templates in figures 3.3 and 3.4 to assist them as they move through these steps and plan with teachers to help them set professional growth goals. Figure 3.3 is provided for coaches who plan to ask specific questions to guide teachers, while figure 3.4 provides a template for coaches who choose to present information or make specific statements in their goal-planning work with teachers. These templates include sample information that has been filled in. You may choose to alter these questions and statements to best suit your situation.

Goal-Planning Steps	Specific Questions
Set general goal areas.	What are the general areas you want to work on this year?
Identify or narrow specific focus of goal.	Within the general goal areas you identified, where do you specifically want to focus? What specifically do you want to accomplish within these areas?
Identify specific components needed to implement goal.	In order to accomplish your specific professional growth goal, what activities will you need to complete, what professional development will you complete, and what will be your timeline to get started?
Choose data or information to assess progress related to goal or attainment of goal.	What data do you plan to gather to assess your progress on this goal? What data will you gather to measure your success in attaining the goal?
Determine peer coach's role.	What would you like me to do to help you implement this goal?
Use this section to write any notes, pertinent information, and so on that will help you assist the teacher in implementing the professional growth goal.	

Figure 3.3: Sample completed goal-setting template for asking questions.

*Visit **go.solution-tree.com/leadership** for a reproducible version of this figure.*

Goal-Planning Steps	Specific Statements
Set general goal areas.	You've mentioned that you want to improve the involvement of the students. That seems like a good area to focus on during this goal cycle.
Identify or narrow specific focus of goal.	To improve the involvement of students, it might help to specifically focus on increasing the use of processing strategies within your classroom. It may be good to try to implement three or four processing activities during each lesson.
Identify specific components needed to implement goal.	In order to implement this goal, I suggest that you observe two other teachers implementing involvement activities, attend a seminar that is scheduled in October, and discuss possible strategies within your collaborative team time.
Choose data or information to assess progress related to goal or attainment of goal.	In order to assess your progress, you could record the involvement strategies you implement and how they have worked in your professional journal. Take a few minutes each week to review your journal.
Determine peer coach's role.	As your peer coach, I'll meet with you every two weeks to discuss how things are going. I'll also complete two observations and provide feedback to you each quarter. We can discuss your progress whenever you would like.
Use this section to write any notes, pertinent information, and so on that will help you assist the teacher in implementing the professional growth goal.	

Figure 3.4: Sample completed goal-setting template for providing information.

*Visit **go.solution-tree.com/leadership** for a reproducible version of this figure.*

Coaching Skills

In order to effectively coach others, a core set of skills is helpful. If you are a leader who supports peer coaches, you will want to share the following skills with your coaches; if you use coaching strategies in your supervision of teachers, consider these strategies for your own use.

▸ Developing trust and rapport

▸ Listening

▸ Paraphrasing and reflecting

- Understanding the coachee and his or her unique perspective
- Using stances
- Designing good questions
- Setting parameters for coaching conferences and conversations
- Conducting conversations throughout the peer coaching cycle
- Using conferencing strategies after observations or at the end of the peer coaching cycle

Developing Trust and Rapport

An essential skill for peer coaches is the ability to develop a professional relationship with the people they are coaching. Trust and a good rapport are necessary for this relationship to be productive because coaches and coachees must work together closely and rely on one another. John Eller and Howard Carlson (2009) explain that "looking at another person while you are speaking to them, sincerely smiling when something interests you, showing personal regard to another" (p. 63) are indicators of a relationship with good rapport, and "the elements of integrity, reliability, honesty, competence, and personal regard work together to help you develop a sense of trust with another person" (p. 63).

Listening

An effective way coaches can build rapport with the teachers they coach is to listen rather than tell during coaching conversations. This foundational skill is necessary for coaches to truly understand what the coachee is saying. Listening is important because it helps the coachee talk through his or her ideas to solve problems and develop new ideas and strategies. An effective coach is able to withhold advice temporarily in order to truly listen to the person he or she is coaching to see what the coachee actually needs. This skill is called *temporary suspension of opinion*. Suspension of opinion helps ensure that you're fully listening to others while they're speaking rather than mentally forming a response. This foundational coaching skill also helps build a positive working relationship and rapport.

Paraphrasing and Reflecting

Another strategy that coaches find effective is to paraphrase what was discussed and reflect on their coaching conferences. Essentially, paraphrased statements summarize major points discussed in a meeting or conference.

By paraphrasing, coaches acknowledge what the other person in the conversation said. This acknowledgment and rephrasing communicates that the coach is listening and heard what the coachee said. Being heard is an important part of effective communication.

In some instances, however, we have noticed that some people are sensitive to being paraphrased. When they hear phrases such as "So, what I think I hear you saying..." or "It's my perception that you were trying to tell us...," they know a paraphrase is coming. This can be a turnoff. Thus, some coaches are finding success by using more clear and direct acknowledgments, a practice called reflecting. Reflecting statements are similar to paraphrases but are more direct.

We use several paraphrasing and reflecting statement types in our work with others. We focus on the following three types (Eller & Carlson, 2009).

1. **Content:** In delivering a content reflection, a coach takes in the statement, then restates the core of the message in a slightly different way. For example, if a coach heard a teacher say, "I ran into trouble when I put the students into small groups to work on a project," the coach might reply, "The lesson went well until the small-group time." By reflecting back the message in a slightly different way, the coach communicates understanding and acknowledges what the teacher said. Following are some sample content reflecting statements.

    ▸ "You shared the three main issues you thought were a problem."

    ▸ "Your major concerns are the students' lack of interest and trying to help them learn."

    ▸ "You said you don't think your students like to be held accountable for their learning."

2. **Emotional:** In emotional reflecting, the coach makes a statement about emotions he or she perceives the coachee is feeling. We can perceive emotion in another person's statement by listening to the tone, intensity, or implication in the message. For example, if the person being coached says, "I don't think the students appreciate the work that I do to help them learn!" the coach might hear the frustration implicit in the statement. The coach could reflect, "You are frustrated by the students' lack of appreciation." Following are some sample emotional reflecting statements.

    ▸ "This situation is very upsetting to you."

> ▸ "You are stressed about your upcoming formal observation."

> ▸ "You are frustrated by the lack of materials you have been provided to teach this unit."

3. **Inferential:** Inferential reflecting is summing up or providing a label for several ideas or issues the teacher presented. For example, if a teacher said, "I always get the challenging students, I never get enough funds for the materials I need to use, and my supervisor is always asking me to change how I teach," the coach may infer that the teacher feels the supervisor lacks respect for him or her. The coach might reflect, "You aren't getting fair treatment by your supervisor."

In developing an inferential reflection, the coach has to listen to the instances provided in the statement and determine what they may have in common. Once the coach has had a chance to think about the common aspects, she can deliver the reflection statement that sums up or identifies the theme for the issues. As you read the following sample statements, think about the issues they might be summarizing for the teacher.

> ▸ "You mentioned several issues that all relate to how you are perceived by your peers."

> ▸ "The first idea you shared was the lack of respect from the parents. The second was how you are always behind in your work. Both of these relate to the pressure you are feeling in your job right now."

> ▸ "In general, the aspects you shared have all contributed to your level of stress."

These types of reflecting statements help coaches quickly and efficiently communicate the understanding of the original statements and provide acknowledgment for the teacher who made the original statement. Reflecting can be a helpful practice to use when working with teachers as a supervisor, as a peer coach, or if you support peer coaches who are working with other teachers.

Understanding the Coachee and His or Her Unique Perspective

Another skill crucial for coaching success is the ability to understand the unique perspective the coachee brings to the experience. We call this perspective a *frame of reference*. People begin to draw conclusions about the world around them based on their experiences. Their experiences, in turn, reinforce their conclusions and solidify their worldview. The frame of reference they develop creates the lens through which they view experiences; it influences their perceptions and expectations. Eller and Carlson (2009) explain:

> Establishing ways of thinking or frames of reference is a natural process and works both to our benefit and detriment. On the positive side, if we weren't able to develop patterns of thinking, we would have to re-learn a lot of the behaviors that we do seemingly without thinking each day. On the negative side, once people become comfortable with their way of thinking or frame of reference, it can be difficult for them to see another perspective or way of thinking. The investment they have in the frame of reference can cause them to "dig in" on issues when they conflict with how they see the world. (pp. 146–148)

Understanding a teacher's frame of reference is essential when coaching. With that information, the coach will have a context for the coachee's actions and will be more aware of techniques the coachee has tried in the past.

By approaching coaching in a way that helps coachees solve an issue—rather than just telling them what to do—coaches create opportunities for the coachee to have new experiences that can alter his or her frame of reference, thus helping them develop a new outlook in a way that encourages future success. Understanding a teacher's frame of reference also helps coaches determine the coaching stance to use in their work with a teacher.

Using Stances

In their book *Mentoring Matters: A Practical Guide to Learning-Focused Relationships*, Laura Lipton and Bruce Wellman (2003) describe skills essential to the mentoring process. They call these skills *mentoring stances*. Since mentoring and coaching are closely related, we have adapted this information for our work as coaches and refer to these stances as *coaching stances*.

Coaches need to be ready to serve their coachees by changing their strategies based on the expressed needs of the coachees, so the stance—or approach—that a coach takes depends on the needs of the coachee and falls on a continuum based on the level of intensity the coachee requires. One job of the coach is to help the coachee determine what type of interaction is needed for his or her specific situation. Following is a brief description of each of the stances and the needs it fills for the coachees.

▸ **Consult:** Using the consult stance, the coach provides needed information to the coachee. This stance helps coachees gain information, understand its application to their goal areas, and get clarification about procedures and policies. This interaction model is helpful for new employees or employees new to a position or process.

▸ **Collaborate:** Using the collaborate stance, the coach works with the coachee to collectively and cooperatively determine a focus and solve problems. In the collaborate stance, the assumption is that the coach and the coachee each bring a contribution to the question or situation. This stance may be used on a limited basis at first but may increase as the coachee becomes more confident and self-reliant.

▸ **Guide:** In the guide stance, the coach tries to guide the thinking of the coachees by asking questions and causing critical reflection rather than just telling coachees what to do. One purpose of guiding is to help the coachee engage in thinking and processing situations and information. This stance is used on a limited basis with new employees but may be used more as these people gain information and experiences.

Coaching stances are useful because they help coaches determine how best to work with the people they are coaching to ensure they are meeting their needs. These stances also allow coaches to tailor the approach to align to those needs. For example, if a coach is working with someone who has a lot of knowledge but could benefit from thinking and reflecting about their practice, then the guide stance might be most helpful. If a coach is working with someone who might benefit from additional ideas, strategies, or techniques, the best approach would be to use the consult stance.

Another way to determine the proper stance to use is to ask the coachee what he or she thinks might be most helpful. Sometimes, coaches are reluctant to ask the person they are coaching what he or she is looking for in the coaching interaction. A simple question like, "As I work with you today, would you like me to provide you with information or ask you questions to help you identify your own ideas?" communicates that the coach is interested in using the coaching stance that best meets the coachee's needs in order to maximize the coaching experience.

Designing Good Questions

When designing good questions, it is important to think about the wording within the question. When coaches use specific phrasing, they help set the stage and guide the thinking of the coachees. Open-ended questions, for instance, allow for any number of responses. For example, if we ask a person to respond to the prompt, "Describe your thoughts about the lesson," we are asking him or her to provide a detailed response where there is no correct answer.

A closed-ended question, on the other hand, requires the person answering to provide a shorter, focused, or defined answer. Many closed-ended questions imply there is a correct answer. For example, a closed-ended question like, "Did you notice what the students did when you showed the video in class?" or "Would you rather start a lesson with a warm-up activity or a review from yesterday's lesson?" communicates to the coachee that he or she needs to provide a defined answer.

Following are some examples of questions with open-ended, empowering wording that invites detail from the person responding (Eller, 2004). Try to integrate this type of phrasing into your work with teachers.

- ▶ "What are your plans to address this situation?"
- ▶ "Share your next steps for working to solve this issue."
- ▶ "Share your ideas for moving forward to address the situation."
- ▶ "What did you notice when you walked to the back of the classroom?"
- ▶ "What did you observe that led you to the conclusion that the lesson was not as effective as you would have liked?"
- ▶ "How will what you observed impact your future work with this group?"

In coaching conversations, coaches want to help coachees expand their thoughts, so open-ended questions are the more desirable choice. Open-ended questions cause the coachee to think in a wider or divergent manner. They also allow the coachee to share his or her thoughts without feeling like he or she is being judged.

Setting Parameters for Coaching Conferences and Conversations

Coaching conversations need to be kept focused and productive. As a coach, you will want to use a strategy called *framing* to help you set the parameters at the beginning of the conversation and bring the conversation back to the topic if it strays during the conference. The skill of framing allows the speaker to set a verbal boundary for the conference and helps bring the conference back on track if the coachee wanders during the conversation. Eller (2004) provides examples of framing statements.

▸ "As we work together today, we need to make sure that our discussion focuses on ideas that we will want to consider for . . ."

▸ "Our [conversation] keeps getting off track because we are looking at the obstacles to [your] work. What we need to focus on right now are the potential benefits of what we are doing. At the end of [our meeting], we can look at those issues that will hinder our progress." (p. 61)

The following guidelines for framing statements are also provided by Eller (2004).

▸ Start using framing as a strategy that will be incorporated in the beginning of a meeting.

▸ Think about the perspectives that the participants will be bringing to the meeting. Try to imagine what distractions from the posted agenda content could take them off track.

▸ Plan an opening that sets the parameters for the meeting. Design statements that will establish these parameters, such as

  ▸ "Today we are here to talk about . . ."

  ▸ "The major points we need to address are . . ."

  ▸ "As we work together, we need to . . ."

  ▸ "Even though there are other new topics that could be addressed in our meeting, we need to focus on . . ."

  ▸ "At our last meeting, we got off track because of . . . In this meeting, we need to get . . ."

  ▸ "Since we have limited time and personal energy, we are going to make sure that we stay on . . ." (p. 62)

Conducting Conversations Throughout the Peer Coaching Cycle

Once the initial goal-setting process has been completed, you will conduct periodic visits and conferences with your coachee. In some cases, these continued observations and coaching sessions will fit naturally into the teacher's goal plan. In other cases, you may have to proactively follow through on a regular basis.

While most coaching conversations will be very natural interactions, it is a good idea to have a guide or planning map to help make conversations flow smoothly. Consider the following steps in planning ongoing coaching conversations.

1. Set a tone for the conversation. For example, "I'm glad we had a chance to get together and talk about your professional growth goals."

2. Overview the conversation or conference. For example, "Today, as we talk, I'd like you to share how things have been going for you in the last two weeks, what kinds of issues you have faced, and any questions you have for me. I will give you some places you can go to get your questions addressed. At the end of our conversation, we'll set up another time to meet later in the month."

3. Ask the coachee to outline his or her progress, situation, or question. For example, "Please take a few minutes to update me on your progress related to _____ over the last two weeks."

4. Provide feedback, strategies, or ideas to help the coachee address his or her progress, situation, or question. For example, "As you look for information on _____, you may consider checking in with _____. If _____ can't help you, ask _____ to give you some idea of who else may be able to provide you with the information."

5. Check to make sure the coachee understands the feedback and has developed a plan to move forward regarding the question or situation posed in the meeting. For example, "What do you think are your next steps in finding out more about _____? What questions do you have about the process?"

6. Set a follow-up meeting date. For example, "Do you want to set a time to meet later in the month, or do you want to just contact me when you feel a need to meet?"

Visit **go.solution-tree.com/leadership** for a blank planning template for continued coaching conversations.

Using Conferencing Strategies After Observations or at the End of the Peer Coaching Cycle

As a peer coach, you'll need to meet with teachers after you conduct an observation to help them reflect on the experience. In some cases, you'll be providing feedback about what you've observed (depending on the coaching stance you use), but it is more effective if you can have the coachee reflect on what happened and what he or she learned in the experience. Consider using the following format for conducting these conferences when you want the coachee to reflect on his or her own learning. You may find the sample questions helpful in developing a script. Having a script helps you stay on track and deal with issues if any should come up in the conference.

- Ask questions to help the coachee review what happened in the lesson, school year, or other observed event. For example:
  - "In general, how do you think the year went?"
  - "What were your thoughts in relation to the event (or school year or lesson) I saw?"
  - "Share with me your overall impressions of the event (or school year or lesson)."
  - "What do you think are the major events that shaped your goals?"

- Ask questions that help the coachee identify things that went well and areas that didn't go so well in the lesson, school year, or observed event. For example:
  - "What specifically happened that told you the event (or year or lesson) was successful?"
  - "What indicators did you use to form your impression that the event (or year or lesson) was successful (or unsuccessful)?"
  - "If you could label two or three things that you used to draw your conclusions about the success of the event (or year or lesson), what would they be?"
  - "How do you know that you were successful (or unsuccessful)? What indicators did you draw on for your conclusions?"

- Ask the coachee to share what he or she observed in the lesson that provides evidence for his or her impressions of the lesson or other observed event. For example:
  - "Why do you think things turned out the way they did?"
  - "What do you think caused the outcome that you observed?"
  - "What was the impact of that event (or statement, strategy, and so on)?"
  - "What did you see as a result of what you did?"

▶ Ask the coachee to share what he or she learned from the experience and how he or she plans to use this learning in future situations. For example:

   ▸ "In this conference, we talked about a lot of ideas. How will you use what you've learned in similar situations in the future?"

   ▸ "What did you learn as a result of our discussion? How will you use that learning?"

   ▸ "Share with me your plan to use what you learned to avoid this kind of situation in the future."

   ▸ "How do you plan to change _____ as a result of what you learned today?"

▶ Ask the coachee what you did as a coach to help him or her and how you can improve your coaching. For example:

   ▸ "How has my coaching assisted you in the process of examining your performance?"

   ▸ "What did I do to help you? What did I do that got in your way?"

   ▸ "How do we want to refine the coaching relationship for the future so you can continue to grow and learn?"

   ▸ "What did I do that assisted you in examining your professional practice? What do I need to refine as a coach for the future?"

Visit **go.solution-tree.com/leadership** for a reproducible template to help you develop your script and plan coaching conversations that take place after an observation or at the end of the peer coaching cycle.

A Look Back

At the start of this chapter, we met Tanya and Bill. When Tanya reviewed and compared the information she received from Bill's coaching session with her goal-setting process template, she saw that she was right on track with her goal plan. Bill's coaching was instrumental in helping her successfully implement her growth goal. She decided that she would update her plan and engage Bill in helping her reach the next stage of the process.

She scheduled a follow-up meeting with Bill and explained her updated focus. Bill asked her to update him on her progress and helped Tanya decide what she would try to accomplish during the second half of the school year. Bill and Tanya then set up a new coaching plan for the remainder of the year.

Chapter Summary

In this chapter, we have discussed several elements of peer coaching. Getting peers involved in observing and providing other teachers with feedback is a central aspect of many of the evaluation requirements set by states in their new teacher evaluation laws. Serving as a peer coach can be a challenging experience. The ideas, skills, and strategies that we have presented in this chapter will make the process more manageable.

As you reflect on the information you learned in this chapter, respond to the following questions.

- ▸ What are some of the unique aspects of being a peer coach?

- ▸ Why are developing a relationship and building rapport important in the coaching process? What are strategies that can help develop a sound coaching relationship?

- ▸ What are some of the attributes of a professional growth goal? Why is being clear and specific important in setting a professional growth goal?

Now that you have had a chance to learn about and reflect on peer coaching, we hope you will find it an effective method for peers to share ideas and help each other grow professionally.

In chapter 4, you will read about strategies to help you gather and use data from teachers' PLC involvement to help them grow. As you review this information, keep in mind that you will need to tie these data back to the teaching performance standards.

Using PLC Information

Ken, a high school principal, was getting ready to meet with Ramon, a mathematics teacher in his building, to decide the focus for his teacher evaluation process this year. Ramon is a continuing-contract teacher who has worked with Ken for ten years. In the past, Ken has conducted observations in Ramon's classroom and provided him with feedback about his teaching skills. Ken found that he has nothing new to share with Ramon when he observes his teaching.

For the upcoming cycle, Ken and Ramon planned to try something new. The school had been working as a professional learning community for three years to try to increase the success of students. This PLC set goals and offered extra help sessions for students, provided new instructional strategies that teachers could use to better develop skills in their students, and identified resources that present concepts in a variety of ways that teachers can use in their classrooms. Ken and Ramon decided to include Ramon's work on the PLC goals as a part of his professional growth and evaluation process. Neither person had done this before, but they were sure that with open communication and collaboration they could make it work.

The situation Ken and Ramon faced is becoming more common in schools as teachers and principals work together to implement new teacher evaluation processes. This chapter will focus on including PLC work as a part of the teacher evaluation process.

Chapter Focus

In this chapter, you will learn more about PLCs, why the work of teachers in PLCs is important to include in the teacher growth and evaluation process, how this can be done, and some of the advantages and challenges of using PLC work in the process. The chapter provides the following.

▸ Considerations for using PLC data, including how the teacher growth and evaluation process interacts with PLC work

▸ A detailed example of one district's integration of PLC work as a part of the teacher growth and evaluation process

As you review this chapter, you'll be reminded of the importance of seeing the total performance of the teacher—not just classroom observations. You'll see how expanding the data used in appraising the teacher's performance will provide you with a more complete and comprehensive picture.

Considerations for Using PLC Data

As we noted in chapter 1, the work of PLCs is one of the alternative data sources a supervisor can use to gain a comprehensive understanding of a teacher's work (see figure 1.2 on page 15 for a reminder of how PLC information can factor in with several other types of data in the evaluation and supervision of teachers). In some schools, PLC work is deeply embedded and is connected to core operations. In other schools, teachers are just getting introduced to the concept and learning how to work together as a PLC. Obviously, the importance or weight the PLC process has in the teacher growth and evaluation process will depend, in part, on the exact stage of the PLC implementation present in the school, the teachers' confidence in being part of a PLC, and the teachers' comfort in using PLC data in their professional growth and evaluation process.

How PLC Work and the Teacher Growth and Evaluation Process Complement Each Other

As schools work to meet the social, emotional, and academic needs of students, the PLC provides teachers with the support they need to improve their practice. A PLC creates an environment where teachers have the opportunity to collaborate and develop their practice by having meaningful conversations about standards, curriculum, instruction, assessments, and performance. As teachers work to support one another and the students within the PLC, they grow in their profession, which is the ultimate goal of a teacher growth and evaluation system. The collective accountability within the PLC helps create a culture that encourages continuous growth and development while also providing the structure to support the work. Similarly, evaluation systems that focus on growth and development will create a culture that supports collaboration. The PLC is one vehicle for evaluation and a place for principals to gather data reflecting the work teachers do to improve student achievement.

Advantages and Challenges of Using PLC Work in the Teacher Growth and Evaluation Process

In thinking about including PLC work as a part of the teacher growth and evaluation process, there are strengths and challenges that a school or district must consider. As we have worked with schools and districts to incorporate PLC data into the teacher growth and evaluation process, these schools have done a cost-benefit analysis to see if the advantages outweigh the challenges of using such an approach. Some of the major advantages and challenges we have encountered are highlighted in table 4.1.

Table 4.1: Possible Benefits and Challenges of Including PLC Work as Part of a Teacher's Growth and Evaluation Process

Benefits	Challenges
• The growth and evaluation process reflects a more comprehensive array of data than just conducting classroom observations.	• Teachers and administrators may not have had extensive experience in using data outside of classroom observations for teacher evaluation and supervision.
• The use of PLC work helps principals address the expectation of collaboration in the growth and evaluation process. This is an attribute that is hard to observe in traditional evaluation systems.	• A part of an individual teacher's growth and evaluation is based on the work of the PLC; this might be hard to measure.
• Including PLC work in teacher growth and evaluation processes communicates its importance to teachers.	• Using the PLC work in the teacher evaluation process requires regular communication, monitoring progress, and making adjustments in the PLC plan. The feedback becomes more fluid and not cut and dry. Some of these processes may be challenging for both the supervisor and the teacher.
• Including PLC work allows supervisors to monitor school-improvement efforts, the use of student achievement data, the implementation of goals, and other aspects of school improvement and student achievement processes.	• The administrator and teacher have to agree on the weighting of the PLC in relation to the other data components in the growth and evaluation process.

It's important to hold open dialogue with teachers about the use of PLC information in the teacher evaluation process. By holding open conversations about the process, you will ensure that it has the clear focus and the adaptability to work in your unique setting. The following section shares the story of a district that uses teachers' participation in their PLC as a part of their teacher growth and evaluation process.

A District's Integration of PLC Work in Teacher Growth and Evaluation

A district we recently worked with has connected its teacher evaluation process with an increased focus on working as a PLC to improve learning opportunities for students. Revising this district's teacher evaluation process in this way was one step toward the district's commitment to ensure that race, class, disability, the school a student attends, or the teacher a student is assigned are no longer the predictors of academic success. The district named this commitment their Equity Promise, and it became the vision to which it would align its PLC work.

The implementation of the district's new teacher development and appraisal process (TDAP) coincided with an effort to identify common priority standards for all grade levels. The previous focus on developing and improving the instruction of individual teachers had minimal influence on the culture of teaching and learning in the district; the intentional focus on evaluating the effectiveness of teacher collaboration amounted to a major investment in teaching strategies, professional growth activities, time to work together in PLCs, and other strategies designed to improve professional interactions and relationships. This work amplified teachers' awareness of the district's shift to a standards-based system of teaching and learning.

Implementation of a Collaborative Approach to Improving Teacher Effectiveness

The district's TDAP was created to increase student learning by improving teacher collaboration within PLCs. Educator, author, and consultant Timothy Kanold (2011) contends that when teachers work in a culture of collaboration, they move from a top-down, compliancy-based mindset to having a greater sense of social motivation. Implementation began with site-based grade-level or job-alike pilot teams and a renewed, well-communicated, districtwide focus on teacher collaboration. Every teacher was presented with an overview of the three big ideas of a PLC (DuFour, DuFour, Eaker, & Many, 2010). The first big idea involves a systemic shift to visible learning whereby students' mastery of standards drives teachers while teachers simultaneously work to become critical evaluators of their effect on student learning. The second big idea is that to achieve higher levels of learning, teachers must work interdependently and begin to view each other as learning resources. The third big idea involves a focus on results.

The district reinforced the mindset that to reach its Equity Promise, each school needed to develop a culture of collaboration whereby teachers move from a mindset of *doing* PLC to one of *being* a PLC (DuFour et al., 2010). A key emphasis for the district in its work to create a collaborative and vibrant learning culture for all was to build shared knowledge around what it means for teachers to be aligned in their work; adopt common, equitable grading practices with inter-rater reliability; and develop a common understanding of the effective components of a well-developed lesson plan. This definition of PLC alignment was a part of a larger attempt to build common knowledge for many new terms that teams would benefit from knowing. The district developed a comprehensive list of terms and embedded it within each school's portfolio as a resource for teachers in need of clarification.

The Plan-Do-Study-Act Cycle of Teaching and Learning

Authors Richard DuFour and Robert J. Marzano (2011) write that PLCs must engage in a recurring cycle of collective inquiry that begins by clarifying what students are to learn. This cycle of teaching and learning came to be known to teachers as Plan-Do-Study-Act (PDSA). In the PDSA cycle, once teams are determined, they work collaboratively to plan instruction (plan), implement their plan (do), track student understanding with commonly developed formative assessments (study), and use evidence from those assessments to collectively identify and eradicate gaps in student understanding (act). In addition to an explanation of the work within each phase of the PDSA cycle, teachers were encouraged to collectively utilize graphic organizers to facilitate planning and implementation and to provide guidance for observing and studying achievement data for the purpose of creating an action plan.

A Self-Evaluation Rubric

As part of the process for appraising and developing teachers, the district created a rubric that teams use to self-assess the effectiveness of their collaboration. Based on the many reproducible tools included in Richard DuFour, Rebecca DuFour, Robert Eaker, and Thomas Many's (2010) book *Learning by Doing*, the rubric helps collaborative teams take inventory of their current reality within three indicators: (1) creating shared norms, (2) setting and monitoring goals, and (3) focusing on results. Once teams determine whether they're in the *initiating, implementing, refining,* or *sustaining* stage within each indicator, the rubric provides possible next steps teams can take to continually improve the impact their collaboration has on student learning. The goal for each team is to progress toward the sustaining column on the rubric. Teams functioning in the sustaining stage of all three indicators have fully embraced learning and collaboration. Their norms allow for them to have frequent, honest, and open conversations around data. When asked, each member can articulate his or her norms, and all members contribute to the creation of meeting agendas and come to meetings prepared to participate in discussion. Each member is a critical evaluator of his or her own student learning, views fellow teachers as learning resources, and adopts a mantra that he or she will do whatever it takes to ensure that students learn.

Processes for Connecting PLC Work to Teacher Evaluation

The PLC process and its application to teaching are the focus of the teacher evaluation process every year for every teacher in the district. The principal, as evaluator, gathers data through conference meetings in the fall, at midyear, and at the end of the year. These three interactive feedback meetings focus on observations of teacher involvement and participation in the PLC, an analysis of the teacher's SMART goals, information shared in building-level meetings, group conversations, walkthroughs, and formal and informal classroom observations. At the end-of-the-year conference, the supervisor provides written feedback to the teacher based on the results of the meetings, the progress of the PLC, and what the teacher has contributed to the success of the PLC through his or her actions.

In addition to the conference meetings with the principal, the teachers also use several tools to facilitate reflection on their PLC work, including the following.

▸ **A digital portfolio during the year that will be shared with the principal:** The portfolio should include all paperwork related to the evaluation process. The portfolio may contain additional documents to support teachers' professional development, their work in the PLC, and artifacts related to their professional growth to highlight in conversations with the principal.

▸ **Samples of the teachers' work with their collaborative teams to develop SMART goals and a PLC goal-setting plan:** The teachers will work within their teams to implement their PLC goal-setting plan. The teachers will—

  ▸ Follow the timeline and identified strategies to attain goals

  ▸ Complete a self-reflection form and discuss it with the principal

  ▸ Collect evidence in their digital portfolios of attainment of goals, such as the following.

   ▸ Assessment reports and indication of progress toward goal

   ▸ PDSA documents

   ▸ Minutes from collaborative team meetings

   ▸ Walkthrough feedback

   ▸ Formal and informal observation reports

   ▸ Professional development activity records

  ▸ Meet with principal as requested for clarification, discussion, and follow-up

▸ **Goals and the PLC plan:** These will be reviewed during the three interactive feedback meetings with the principal's designee.

▸ **Improvement plans:** If a teacher does not meet the district requirements, the process could include greater involvement from administrators and additional improvement plans.

▸ **End-of-the-year summary:** This is completed by the principal or designee following a discussion with the teacher regarding progress made during the year on his or her professional goal as defined in the PLC goal-setting plan.

A Timeline for the Teacher Development and Evaluation Process

The district developed a timeline (see figure 4.1, pages 78–80) to help guide the process for teacher development and evaluation. You may find this information helpful as you think about including the work of your PLC in the teacher evaluation process.

August/September

Building Leadership Team

- Establish overall building goals/parameters
- Set professional development opportunities

Professional Learning Community (PLC)

- Establish norms and clarify expectations of how team will operate
- Develop SMART goals
- Create strategies to attain goals
- Identify professional development needs
- Ongoing refinement of strategies/assessments
- Schedule conference meeting days

Teachers

- Implement strategies/assessments
- Monitor and adjust strategies/process
- Work with the PLC to refine strategies/assessments

Principals/Administrators/Trained Evaluators

- Work with leadership teams to establish overall goals
- Review SMART goals for each PLC
- Work with leadership team to refine SMART goals
- Schedule point of contact days
- Initiate walk-throughs and continue throughout the year

November

Professional Learning Community (PLC)

- Review student progress towards goals
- Modify professional development plan
- Meet with principal to review student progress and/or create action/follow-up plan
- Work toward the sustaining level on the rubric

Teachers

- Review student progress towards goals
- Monitor and adjust strategies towards achieving the goals
- Work with the PLC to refine strategies/assessments

Principals/Administrators/Trained Evaluators

- Initiate conference with the PLC
- Create an action plan with individual teachers/PLCs who need additional support
- Follow up with teams/individuals on implementation of action plan

- Continue walk-throughs
- Work with PLC on progress towards the sustaining level on the rubric

January

Professional Learning Community (PLC)

- Review student progress towards goals
- Modify professional development plan
- Meet with principal to review student progress and/or create action/follow-up plan
- Work towards the sustaining level on the rubric

Teachers

- Review student progress towards goals
- Modify professional development plan
- Meet with principal to review student progress and/or create action/follow-up plan
- Work towards the sustaining level on the rubric

Principals/Administrators/Trained Evaluators

- Initiate conference meeting #2 with the PLC
- Create an action plan with individual teachers/PLCs who need additional support
- Follow up with teams/individuals on implementation of action plan
- Continue walkthroughs
- Work with PLC on progress towards the sustaining level on the rubric

April

Professional Learning Community (PLC)

- Review student progress towards goals
- Modify professional development plan
- Meet with principal to review student progress and/or create action/follow-up plan

Teachers

- Review student progress towards goals
- Monitor and adjust strategies towards achieving the goals
- Work with the PLC to refine strategies/assessments

Principals/Administrator/Trained Evaluators

- Initiate point of contact #3 with the PLC
- Create an action plan with individual teachers/PLCs who need additional support

Figure 4.1: Timeline for teacher development and evaluation process.

Continued →

> - Follow up with teams/individuals on implementation of action plan
> - Continue walkthroughs
>
> **May**
>
> Professional Learning Community (PLC)
>
> - Goal reflection / summative evaluation due in May

Source: Mounds View Public Schools. Used with permission.

Several features are prevalent in this timeline. As you can see, there are several other structures working collaboratively with the PLC to coordinate the school improvement process. The administration and the building-level instructional leadership teams provide direction and coordination for the work of the PLC. The individual teacher's responsibilities are also designated in the timeline.

Key Aspects and Ideas to Consider

For your convenience, we have highlighted key aspects of the district's model that we recommend focusing on when connecting PLC work and teacher evaluation in your schools.

▸ Emphasize the positive aspects of both the PLC process and the teacher evaluation process. If you focus on the good instead of the negative, your teachers will have a positive and engaging process. If you penalize them for moving too slowly or not reaching their goals, you'll quickly turn them off to the process.

▸ Keep in mind that your PLC will go through several stages as your staff learn how to work together. Typically, teams work during the first year of the PLC process to learn how to collaborate and develop some common directions. Keep this in mind as you think about using PLC work in your teacher evaluation process.

▸ Since you are looking at some data related to the work products of the entire PLC, it may be harder for you to focus on the productivity of a single member of the group. You may want to work with those individuals to find ways to document their unique contributions to the PLC process.

See appendix A (page 183) for a collection of forms and templates to use as guides as you begin to coordinate the PLC process and teacher evaluation in your school or district.

A Look Back

At the beginning of the chapter, Ken and Ramon were working together to identify how the work Ramon was doing in his collaborative team might be helpful in the professional growth and evaluation process. Ramon's grade-level collaborative team was going to examine the process of increasing student engagement in the classroom. Both Ken and Ramon thought this might be a good focus for Ramon's professional growth.

As the year progressed, Ramon learned some good strategies that he thought he could implement in his classroom. As he tried some of these, he shared his progress with Ken. These were the same strategies he had discussed with Ken at the beginning of the year and had written into his professional growth plan. After he was more comfortable with his implementation of several of the strategies, he decided to invite Ken into his classroom to observe the strategies in action. After the observation, Ken let Ramon share his perceptions of the effectiveness of the strategies and how much Ramon had learned in the process. Ken suggested that Ramon share the results of his implementation with his grade-level team and with the rest of the faculty at an upcoming meeting. Ramon was happy and excited about his growth and his decision to integrate his PLC work in the teacher growth and evaluation process.

Chapter Summary

In this chapter, we have discussed the use of PLC data in the teacher evaluation process and illustrated how one school district has implemented this practice. This information will be important for you to consider because of the crucial role PLCs play in school improvement and increasing teacher connectedness and collaboration.

As you reflect on the information you learned in this chapter, respond to the following questions.

▸ What are some valid reasons to justify the use of PLC information as a part of the teacher evaluation process?

▸ Why is it important to focus on positive data related to a PLC use when first connecting PLC work to the teacher evaluation process? How can focusing on the positive aspects help your teachers become more receptive to these data and also increase the effectiveness of the PLC?

▸ What are some of the positive aspects you saw in the description of district programs featured in this chapter? How is this information helpful to you as you consider using PLC data as part of your teacher evaluation process?

Using PLC information as a part of the teacher evaluation process holds great promise but needs careful thought and consideration before jumping in. The information presented in this chapter should help you carefully think through this option.

In the next chapter, we will explore another alternative data source, the professional portfolio. This source of data provides information that would otherwise be unavailable to the evaluator and also encourages teachers to be collaborative partners in their evaluations.

chapter 5

Using Portfolios

Fernando, a high school mathematics teacher, always felt he did a good job in the classroom. The students did well on standardized tests, he always had high enrollment in his classes, and several students had come back after graduation to tell him how much they enjoyed his class and how helpful it was to them when they went to college.

Even though Fernando was confident, today he was nervous because he was going to meet with his principal, Allison, to discuss the results of the portfolio he had developed. He had never really thought about capturing evidence about his professional growth and teaching before Allison asked him to do so. He thought through what he had learned in the process and how he was going to share this with her.

Fernando's fears were soon alleviated when he and the principal started their conversation. Allison shared with him that it looked like he had been gathering good evidence about what he was doing in the classroom. Also, much of the information that was in Fernando's portfolio could be used to help him renew his teaching license. The portfolio process could serve two purposes, which Fernando felt actually saved him time and work.

Rather than tell Fernando what to do next in the portfolio process, Allison asked him how he planned to use the information. Fernando shared several ideas with her, and together they developed a plan to follow up on some of the strategies he shared during this conference. He left the office happy and energized to continue to grow as a teacher.

In this scenario, Allison was wise to ask Fernando to begin using this alternative data source. Since she had been working with Fernando for a number of years, she felt like she was always giving him the same feedback again and again. After the start of this year's evaluation cycle, they talked about trying something new—using portfolio data to help Fernando continue to grow as a teacher.

Chapter Focus

In this chapter, we will focus on using portfolios in the evaluation and supervision process to help teachers gain a new perspective and grow as professionals. As you review the information contained in this chapter, you will learn the following.

▸ Components of a professional portfolio

▸ Portfolio planning tips, including strategies and techniques to integrate portfolios into the teacher evaluation process

▸ Steps for conducting meaningful conversations during the completion of the portfolio process

Alternative data sources such as portfolios help teachers see their teaching from a slightly different point of view. They can be motivational for novices as well as master teachers on your staff.

Components of a Professional Portfolio

We have had the opportunity to work with teachers in a variety of settings using portfolios. Simply put, a portfolio is a collection of artifacts that represent activities, events, thoughts, or reflections. Figure 5.1 illustrates how a typical portfolio might be organized.

The two major components normally included in a portfolio are artifacts and reflections. The artifacts, or evidence, are based on teacher goals, organizational priorities, or agreed-on criteria (McLaughlin et al., 1998). Artifacts can take many different forms, depending on the specific teaching standard they are representing. For example, a picture of a teacher with a group of students on a field trip could be used to represent the planning that went into the experience. Examples of student work demonstrating their use of self-assessment strategies could be used to represent a new project idea that a teacher has designed. The first chapter of a master's thesis could be included to demonstrate a professional academic accomplishment on the part of the teacher.

Artifact: *Classroom Roman Empire Projects*	**Reflections**
	Description of the artifact: *The artifact is a picture of students developing projects for a unit on the Roman Empire. I let the students complete projects to show me what they learned in the unit. I had them complete a self-assessment based on a pre-established scoring guide.* Description of what was learned in the experience: *I learned that it can be a good idea to let the students have input into the assessment and learning demonstration. They selected good projects to demonstrate their learning. After reviewing their projects, I determined which content areas I needed to reteach in order to help the students achieve mastery. The students provided that information to me in their self-assessments of the projects.* Description of how the artifact or experience fits into the teaching area: *This artifact fits into the teaching standard "promotes student self-assessment" because I had the students complete a self-reflection related to their projects.* Description of how the teacher plans to use what was learned in the experience for future instruction: *I plan to have the students complete a self-assessment on future assignments.*

Figure 5.1: Example of a completed portfolio entry.

The types of artifacts that can be used to represent learning are unlimited, because artifacts represent the larger accomplishments and learning of a teacher. In some cases, these artifacts are the choice of the teacher, but they can also be mandated by district practices. In general, the portfolio categories or themes should be based on teacher performance standards.

Reflections are the learnings, thoughts, and ideas generated as a result of the activity or experience that the artifact represents. For example, if a teacher has included the first chapter of a master's thesis as an artifact, the reflection for this artifact would describe the teacher's learning in the master's program. There are many models of reflective statements for artifacts, but we find that reflections normally focus on four areas.

1. A description of the artifact or the experience, activity, or strategy represented by the artifact

2. A description of what was learned through the experience or activity represented by the artifact

3. A description of how the artifact or experience, activity, or strategy fits into the teaching performance standards

4. A description of how the teacher plans to use what was learned in the experience, activity, or strategy for future instruction

If you choose to include portfolios in your teacher evaluation processes, give some thought to the types of artifacts that should be included. The type of artifacts will determine the focus of the portfolio. Table 5.1 lists several categories and examples of portfolio artifacts.

As you work with your teachers, you may want to consider other options as long as they fit the requirements of your district. Keep in mind that the artifacts provide evidence of an experience or event while the reflections provide the details of the experience, the teacher's thoughts about the experience, and what the teacher learned as a result of the experience. Both the artifact and the reflection work together to outline the entry in the portfolio that documents the teacher's growth.

Portfolio Planning

At the beginning of the portfolio process, it's a good idea to hold a portfolio planning conference. A portfolio planning conference can help a supervisor work with their teachers to better align the artifacts and reflections in their portfolios to the evaluation priorities of the district or building.

Table 5.1: Artifact Categories and Examples

Categories of Portfolio Artifacts	Examples of Portfolio Artifacts
General	Artifacts related to the general components of the teaching performance standards, such as: • Pictures of student projects documenting that the students were able to demonstrate their learning • Examples of students' work illustrating their mastery of a particular concept • Copies of notes from parents thanking the teacher for the extra effort they gave to make their children successful
Priority Based	Artifacts related to the areas of the teaching performance standards the district or building has deemed as priorities based on student learning needs, such as: • A summary of student test scores documenting growth in priority areas • Examples of lesson plans illustrating the use of differentiated teaching strategies when the district has named this area as a focus • Journal entries documenting the use of student engagement strategies and the teacher's reflections about these strategies
Difficult to Observe	Artifacts related to the teaching performance expectations that are difficult for evaluators to observe, such as: • Professional association activities that the teacher has led • A list of district leadership experiences to illustrate teacher leadership • Syllabi from coursework taken for additional degrees or professional growth
Professional Development Based	Artifacts related to the teaching performance standards and the individual teacher's professional development plan (some may be observable by the evaluator while others may be hard to observe), such as: • Copies of handouts from professional development seminars the teacher has attended • Reflections from the peer coaching experiences the teacher has experienced during their informal evaluation years • Certificates earned as a result of professional development seminar attendance
Relicensure or Recertification Based	Artifacts related to the requirements or standards of state relicensure or recertification, such as: • A copy of the updated teaching license • Certificates from professional development or relicensure seminars attended • Clock-hour certificates for licensure courses attended

A portfolio planning conference should be a collaborative experience between supervisors and teachers. Even though a portfolio planning conference sounds like it might be informal, it should have a clear agenda and purpose. Using a planning form when preparing to conduct a conference can help ensure such clarity. See figure 5.2 for an example of a portfolio planning form.

When using a portfolio as an alternative data source in the evaluation process, supervisors should initially coach teachers rather than direct them. This means that a supervisor should make sure teachers are involved in a collaborative manner rather than telling them what to place in their portfolio, what to include as reflections, and other aspects of their portfolio. By engaging teachers in creating their own portfolios, supervisors help the teacher invest

Portfolio Planning Form

Use the following form to plan the specific focus of your portfolio. Also use this form to plan some of the artifacts that you will include in your portfolio.

Name: _Sample_ Subject or grade level: _Science_

Evaluator: _Sample_ Date: _____

Portfolio category (circle one):

General

(Professional development based)

Relicensure or recertification based

Priority based

Difficult to observe

Professional Growth Goal	Artifacts
Professional growth goal area 1: Increase use of student engagement in the classroom	• Certificate from professional development workshop on topic • Reflection on what was learned in professional development workshop • Baseline student engagement level from observation by peer coach • List of strategies implemented in the classroom to improve student engagement • Midyear level of engagement from peer coach observation
Professional growth goal area 2: Work to obtain master's degree in teacher leadership	• Master's program acceptance letter • Syllabi from courses taken in master's program during the school year • Reflection document outlining what has been learned and implemented to date as a result of the master's program • Major assignments and readings from master's program courses • Program of study for courses and thesis completion

Professional Growth Goal	Artifacts
Professional growth goal area 3: Increase comfort and frequency in assuming teacher leadership roles in the building	• Reflections on the major information related to teacher leadership learned in master's program courses • List of leadership roles currently performing on committees and collaborative teams • Plan to increase involvement and leadership activities
Dates for follow-up meetings to discuss the progress of the portfolio: *January 15, March 22, May 10*	

Figure 5.2: Sample portfolio planning form.

*Visit **go.solution-tree.com/leadership** for a reproducible version of this figure.*

in the portfolio. Teachers who are invested in the development of their portfolio will make it more meaningful and detailed, take the process more seriously, and put together a quality portfolio. Teachers who are following the directives or mandates of their supervisors may develop a portfolio that only meets the minimum standards and does not reflect their professional growth.

The following steps are important in coaching a teacher in the development of a portfolio.

1. Ask the teacher to share the desired focus of his or her portfolio.

2. Have the teacher share the themes or major areas he or she plans to focus on in the portfolio.

3. Have the teacher share some of the activities, experiences, and artifacts he or she plans to include in the portfolio.

4. Discuss how you plan to work with the teacher to integrate the portfolio data into the broader teacher evaluation process and the summative evaluation. Get the teacher's ideas, and share any thoughts you may have about this aspect of the evaluation process.

5. Have the teacher share how he or she plans to keep you updated on the progress of the portfolio. Schedule any follow-up meetings you plan to hold.

Supervisors can use these steps to help a teacher grow professionally, and peer coaches can also use them if they are working with a teacher to develop a portfolio as a part of the professional growth process. The steps for ongoing coaching conversations outlined in chapter 3 (page 49) may also be helpful in guiding follow-up conversations throughout portfolio development.

Completion of the Portfolio Process

As supervisors and peer coaches approach the end of the evaluation cycle, they should hold a meeting to discuss what was accomplished in the process, the teacher's perception of the process, and the information from the portfolio that could be used in the summative evaluation. The dialogue in this meeting should be collaborative in nature. The following conversation steps can be used to conduct the end-of-year portfolio conversation.

1. Have the teacher share his or her general impressions of the portfolio process.

2. Have the teacher identify what went well and areas that didn't go so well in relation to the portfolio.

3. Ask the teacher to share what he or she learned in the portfolio process and how he or she plans to implement this learning in future teaching.

4. Ask the teacher to share how he or she thinks the portfolio information could be used in the summative evaluation. Share some thoughts about your perspective on the possible use of the portfolio in the summative evaluation.

5. Thank the teacher for his or her work on the portfolio and for sharing what he or she learned in the process.

A Look Back

At the beginning of this chapter, we introduced you to Fernando, a teacher who was working with his principal, Allison, to develop a portfolio. After their initial meeting, Fernando gathered artifacts that illustrated how he met his professional growth objectives. He also had an opportunity to write some reflections about what he had learned. Since it was getting close to the end of the school year, Fernando was preparing to meet with Allison to discuss his progress for the year.

Allison asked him to reflect on the year and his insights based on the portfolio. Fernando said that he was surprised how much he was doing in relation to his professional growth goal. Keeping track of artifacts and then reflecting on them helped keep the goal in the forefront of his mind. Fernando also said he planned to keep working on his portfolio during the next school year to continue his growth. He thanked his principal for encouraging him to develop a portfolio and for *coaching* him rather than *telling* him during the growth process.

Fernando learned a lot about his teaching as a result of the portfolio. And because Allison allowed him to develop his own thoughts about how to pursue his goals rather than be told what he needed to do, he was able to achieve professional growth.

Keep in mind that portfolios are one of several tools that can be used in the supervision and growth process. In this example, Fernando was already meeting the expectations of the district and was also the type of teacher who could look at data (his portfolio) objectively and grow from the experience. The alternative data source worked well for him. You will encounter other teachers who may need more direction and feedback in their portfolio process. You may need to be more prescriptive about what teachers need to focus on and more directive in discussing the outcome of some of the artifacts in their portfolios, or you may even choose to use different data sources altogether rather than use a portfolio.

Chapter Summary

In this chapter, you learned some basic information about using a teacher-prepared portfolio as a data source in the evaluation process. As we mentioned earlier in the chapter, it's important to try to keep the focus on the positive aspects of the portfolio and the teacher learning that has occurred as a result.

As you reflect on the information you learned in this chapter, respond to the following questions.

▸ Why is it important to hold a planning conference before the teacher starts compiling a portfolio that will be used as a data source for his or her evaluation?

▸ What are the purposes of artifacts in a portfolio? How can you use a teacher's reflections to help him or her determine his or her professional learning?

▸ What considerations need to be taken into account before implementing portfolios as a part of the teacher evaluation process?

In the next chapter, we will examine the use of student feedback in the evaluation process. As we review this idea, keep in mind that student feedback is also an alternative data source. As with other data sources, when using student feedback, it is important to accentuate as many of the positive aspects as possible.

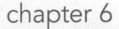

chapter 6

Using Student Feedback

At Adams Elementary School, most of the teachers were doing a good job. However, Robert always seemed to get more out of his students. Those who came into his fourth-grade class not understanding core academic concepts were confident and competent by the end of the school year. Robert's principal, Erin, has watched him teach and has seen how he engages students in his lessons. She has also seen how well he manages his classroom. Parents of students in Robert's class sent Erin notes and talked to her at school events about how happy their children have been in Robert's classroom.

Over the years, Erin pointed out Robert's strengths, but she found herself saying the same things over and over. She wanted to help Robert understand what he's doing right in his classroom by using another data source in addition to her observations.

In their fall planning meeting, Erin suggested that Robert survey his students to find out what they identify as effective in his teaching. Robert thought this was a great idea and worked with Erin to design the survey that he could implement midyear.

After the survey results were complete, Erin and Robert scheduled a meeting to talk about what he learned from his students about his teaching. Robert was quite excited about the results and decided to share the survey information and even use it in the unit he was teaching on graphs.

This story may not seem typical to you, but student feedback related to the learning environment, sometimes referred to as *student engagement strategies*, can be a useful data source to consider when supervising teachers.

These student feedback and perception opportunities can yield highly effective alternative data sources to be used in understanding student perceptions of classroom conditions.

Chapter Focus

In this chapter, we will focus on the following aspects of using student feedback and perceptions in the teacher evaluation process.

▸ Types of student feedback information that make sense for use in the teacher evaluation process

▸ How to plan for the use of student perception data, including a planning conference template to share when meeting with teachers who intend to gather student feedback

▸ Methods for organizing and analyzing the data in order to lead a reflective discussion about student feedback with the teacher

This chapter will help you gather and use this new data source effectively.

Types of Student Feedback Information

Before considering strategies for collecting feedback, it's important to determine the type of information that students can most accurately provide. For instance, students should be able to describe the day-to-day operation of the classroom, the clarity of the content presented, the equity of treatment of students, and the levels of focus and distraction that occur in a normal school day. However, students might be more challenged to actually evaluate their teachers. For example, as students ourselves, many of us have had the experience of working with a very demanding teacher who may have irritated us at the time but who really helped us grow. If we had evaluated the teacher while we were in the classroom, he or she may have received low ratings. In retrospect, as adults, we might rate this teacher much higher. When deciding the focus of student feedback, supervisors need to be careful to focus on areas where the students can provide observable feedback rather than just their opinions about whether they like their teacher.

Once supervisors have selected the proper areas in which students will be asked to provide their feedback, the appropriate instruments can be selected or developed to gather these data. There are a variety of ways we can gather student feedback. We'll share a few in the following sections.

Student Surveys

A student survey consists of questions administered at some point during the course. In some cases, a survey is administered at the beginning of the course and again at the end, and the results are compared. In other situations, a survey is administered only at the end of the course, grading period, semester, and so on. Surveys can be printed on paper or administered electronically. They can also be designed as a series of statements with multiple-choice answers that students choose based on their perception of the reality in the classroom. See figure 6.1 for an example of a possible survey item.

My teacher starts class on time.

1. Always   2. Most of the time   3. Occasionally   4. Seldom   5. Never

---

Figure 6.1: Sample survey item.

Once students have completed the survey, the results are tabulated and the averages are calculated. The supervisor then shares the results with the teacher (or the teacher might tabulate the results and share the information with the supervisor). These results are the basis for a conference.

The supervisor and the teacher need to keep in mind that this is just one source of information that needs to be combined with other data sources like classroom observations, lesson plans, achievement data, and other data to gain a complete picture of a teacher's performance.

Informal Student Feedback

Informal student feedback forms are a little different from student surveys because they ask open-ended questions and the feedback the student provides is narrative or descriptive in nature. Informal student feedback forms normally ask students to respond to several general questions and provide written responses. See figure 6.2 (page 96) for an example of an informal student feedback form.

Informal student feedback is more descriptive than student surveys and may take longer to gather (students will need more time to respond) and require more time to tabulate or determine the summation of the feedback. On the positive side, informal student feedback can also provide very detailed information to help the teacher understand exactly what students perceive is happening in the classroom. The increased level of detail can be helpful in meaningful conversations between supervisors and teachers.

Please take a few minutes to respond to the following questions about your classroom. Your answers are confidential and only the combined responses from all of the students will be shared with your teacher.

1. Please describe how your teacher normally starts class.

2. How does your teacher provide help to students who need extra assistance in class?

3. How much of the class is on task during a typical lesson?

4. Describe how clear your teacher is in explaining the content of your class.

Figure 6.2: Sample informal student feedback form.

Student Interviews and Focus Groups

In some settings, students are interviewed either individually or in small focus groups to gain their perceptions of the learning environment. Interviewers can be administrators, evaluators, school counselors, or possibly another trusted educator. Some schools may even hire professional organizations to conduct these interviews. In implementing interviews or focus groups, it's important for the supervisor to think about the following issues.

▶ The person conducting the interview or focus group needs to have some expertise in asking questions and listening to responses. This person must understand that his or her job is not to put words in the students' mouths.

▶ The information gathered during an interview or focus group could be very sensitive. Confidentiality for both the participants and the teacher is crucial.

▶ Some form of accurate data gathering needs to be in place. Normally, the interviewer or the focus group facilitator writes down what is reported. The data need to reflect the respondents' exact words—not the interpretation of the person conducting the interview or focus group.

▸ This form of data gathering can be very helpful but also very scary for a teacher. Be sure to move forward slowly and use other data sources to gain a perspective of the teacher's complete performance.

Technology-Assisted Feedback

Some teachers use technology to gain feedback on student perceptions of their classroom. Tools such as online surveys (like SurveyMonkey), wikis, and other technology-assisted feedback methods can provide confidential and immediate ways to find out students' perceptions of a classroom.

Each method has strengths and weaknesses. In table 6.1, we provide a summary of the strengths and limitations of each method.

Table 6.1: Pros and Cons of Student Perception Methods

Student Perception Method	Strengths	Limitations
Student survey	• Is concise and efficient • Is confidential • Provides a large amount of general information • Is easily scored or tabulated • Can easily be reflected in a chart or graph	• Information may lack the detail or depth needed to make changes • Method may not work well for younger students • Students may try to complete the survey quickly with little thought and just fill in the blanks • Students may not feel the survey is confidential • Survey only focuses on the areas the school or teacher chooses
Informal student feedback	• Allows for very detailed or descriptive feedback • Lets students share what they think is important	• Takes a lot of time to administer • Takes a lot of time to tabulate and score the results • Students may feel that since they are writing responses, there is a chance of determining who wrote the responses (loss of confidentiality) • There may be some misunderstanding of what kind of feedback is expected

Continued →

Interviews and focus groups	• Allow for very active participation by students • Allow for clarification if responses are vague or general • May give students a sense of importance because of the attention they get in an interview or focus group • Can facilitate a conversation guided by students	• Very time consuming • Loss of confidentiality; students have to state their answers • Tabulating or coming up with data summaries can be time consuming • There may be some inaccuracies in the responses because the interviewer is writing them
Technology-assisted feedback	• Is time efficient, allowing students to complete on their own schedule • Is confidential and anonymous • Is a familiar platform for students	• Requires Internet connection, not always available to students • May result in students saying anything they want—including inappropriate responses—because technology can facilitate anonymity • Depending on the technology resource used, some responses may be visible to other students • May require some technological expertise to set up the feedback tool

You will want to consider these strengths and limitations before you choose to implement a specific data-gathering method.

How to Plan for the Use of Student Feedback Data

It's a good idea to hold a planning conference before gathering student classroom feedback. A planning conference allows supervisors to help teachers focus on the evaluation priorities of the district or building when gathering and analyzing student perception data. This experience should be a collaboration between supervisors and their teachers, with a clear agenda and purpose. Figure 6.3 provides an example of a completed student classroom feedback planning form for use in a planning conference that focuses on collecting student perception data.

When using student feedback about the classroom as an alternative data source in the evaluation process, supervisors will want to initially involve or work in collaboration with their teachers rather than simply direct them in the process. It's important to ensure that teachers are involved in a collaborative manner during the initial implementation of student feedback information.

Student Classroom Feedback Planning Form

Use this form to plan the specific focus for gathering data on student perceptions of the classroom.

Name: _Daniel Rodriguez_   Subject or grade level: _Eighth-grade earth science_

Evaluator: _Marsha Atherton_

Data-gathering method (circle one):

Paper survey

(Electronic survey)

Informal/descriptive

Student interviews

Student focus group interview

Teaching Goals	Possible Questions
Focus on keeping on task in learning activities	• Does the teacher normally start class on time? • Does the teacher normally get back on topic quickly after an off-task response by a student?
Engagement of all students in processing information throughout the lesson	• Does the teacher normally provide a chance for all students to answer the questions posed during instructional portions of the lesson? • Does the teacher normally use pair shares, include small-group processing, ask students to talk to each other, and use other engaging activities as a way for students to process the information during instruction in a class?

Date information will be gathered: _December 17_

Date survey results will be reviewed: _January 5_

Figure 6.3: Sample student classroom feedback planning form.

*Visit **go.solution-tree.com/leadership** for a reproducible version of this figure.*

Consider the following steps for assisting teachers in planning to gather student classroom perception data.

1. Have the teacher share the major areas he or she would like information on during the process of gathering student classroom feedback.

2. Share any areas from the supervision perspective that are crucial in gathering student classroom feedback based on building, district,

or student needs. Also, be sure to include any priorities identified in previous observations or evaluation experiences with the teacher.

3. Discuss how you plan to work with the teacher to integrate the student classroom feedback data into the broader teacher evaluation process and the summative evaluation. Get the teacher's ideas, and share any supervisory thoughts about this aspect of the evaluation process.

4. Discuss the dates during which the data-gathering process will occur. Also discuss when the data will be compiled, when the results will be shared with the teacher, and when a discussion of the data will be scheduled.

Methods for Organizing and Analyzing the Data

Once supervisors have determined what methods to use to obtain student perception data and the data have been gathered, the next step is to compile and analyze the data. When organizing the data, select the method that will provide the clearest picture for both the supervisor and the teacher. In the sections that follow, we present common methods to organize and help in the data-analysis process.

Survey Report

One way to organize the data you collect is through a survey report. Typically, the information in this type of report is organized by themes. Figures 6.4 and 6.5 are from a commercial survey report, but data from student surveys can also be easily reported using Excel or other spreadsheet programs, which provide several tools to generate reports, tables, charts, and graphs. The inclusion of figures 6.4 and 6.5 is not meant to be an endorsement of any particular product or company but rather to provide examples to assist the reader in visualizing a completed report. In figure 6.4, the sample student survey results show that their teacher normally does a good job letting the students know about potential problem areas in course content. If the principal has noticed several students struggling during classroom observations and the testing data show that students are making mistakes applying content, this student survey data could be used to encourage a teacher to spend more time explaining or pointing out the possible areas where errors could occur. Here, the student feedback data may provide a deeper insight into an issue that has been identified in the other data sources.

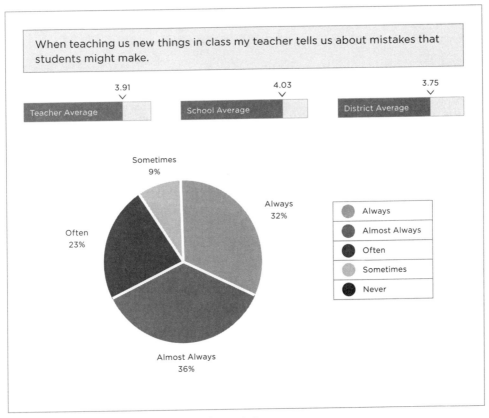

When teaching us new things in class my teacher tells us about mistakes that students might make.

3.91 — Teacher Average

4.03 — School Average

3.75 — District Average

Always 32%

Almost Always 36%

Often 23%

Sometimes 9%

Legend:
- Always
- Almost Always
- Often
- Sometimes
- Never

Source: My Student Survey (2014). Used with permission.

Figure 6.4: Sample student survey results to provide insight into existing data.

In figure 6.5 (page 102), the sample results show that this teacher has received mostly favorable feedback from the students regarding the clarity he or she has provided in explanations. These data could be coupled with observational data (where the principal has observed the teacher clearly explaining concepts) and the results of assessment data showing that the students understand the core aspects of the content. The student perception data act to reinforce the other two data sources.

Informal Feedback Summary

Figure 6.6 (page 103) shows how to organize and report the information from informal student feedback. Once students have finished answering the questions, a person selected by the teacher or supervisor reviews the responses and records the answers to provide the teacher with all the information gathered through the informal surveys. As you review the figure, keep in mind that the information listed is just a summary for illustrative purposes. In a real situation, there would be many more responses.

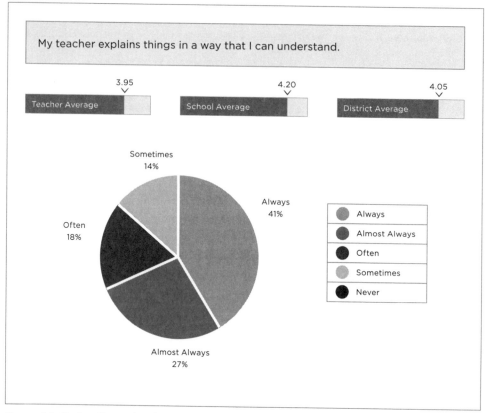

Source: *My Student Survey (2014). Used with permission.*

Figure 6.5: Sample student results to reinforce existing data.

As you look at this information, you can see that it's very detailed in nature. Because it's descriptive and qualitative, there's more room for interpretation. For example, there may be some implied information in the statements in figure 6.6. The statement in which the student says he or she doesn't want to be embarrassed could lead you to believe that there may be a problem with the safety of the learning environment in the classroom. The statement could also be implying that the students really care what the teacher thinks of them, and they don't want to give this teacher a bad impression.

Another way to report informal student feedback is to provide a summary of the trends found in analyzing the responses. An example of this method is provided in figure 6.7 (page 104).

At times, a summary can be helpful because it allows the supervisor and the teacher to quickly examine the main points and decide if they need to look deeper into some of the questions or areas of focus based on the trends of the responses from the students.

Teaching Goal	Question	Student Response Trends
Instructor stays on task	Does your teacher stay focused and on task in the classroom?	• Yes, the teacher reminds us of how much time we have left in class. • I think so. He's always saying, "Let's get back to work." • Sometimes students try to change the topic. He always tells them to get back on track.
Instructor keeps everyone involved during the lesson	Does your instructor keep you involved during the lesson?	• Most of the time. Sometimes the same students try to answer all the questions. • Yes—it's hard to sleep in this class. • Usually—some students don't want to be involved. • He does. You have to pay attention so you don't get embarrassed when you don't know the answer.
Instructor stays on task	Does your teacher stay focused and on task in the classroom?	• Twenty-four (50 percent) of the students said yes. They provided examples of strategies the teacher used to keep the class on task. • Twenty-four (50 percent) of the students said no. They provided examples of when the class was off task and the teacher was unable to get them back on task.
Instructor keeps everyone involved during the lesson	Does your instructor keep you involved during the lesson?	• Ten students said yes and provided examples of activities the teacher has used. • Twenty students said no and that they have drifted off regularly in class. • The remaining students said there are times when they have been engaged and other times when they have become disengaged.

Figure 6.6: Sample informal descriptive feedback summary.

Interview and Focus Group Data Reports

Even though focus group and interview information may be a little different than informal survey information, the reporting and organizational strategies we presented for these methods can also be used for interview data. The supervisor and teacher will need to look at the raw data and decide whether to provide all of the information or provide a summary of the information. Just like the informal feedback reporting, the selection of details should be based on what level of detail might be needed in order to hold a meaningful learning conversation between the teacher and the supervisor. The supervisor and the teacher should look at the general information for trends and then dig deeper until they get the specifics they need to understand the trends.

Teaching Goal	Question	Student Response Trends
Instructor stays on task	Does your teacher stay focused and on task in the classroom?	• Twenty-four (50 percent) of the students said yes. They provided examples of strategies the teacher used to keep the class on task. • Twenty-four (50 percent) of the students said no. They provided examples of when the class was off task and the teacher was unable to get them back on task.
Instructor keeps everyone involved during the lesson	Does your instructor keep you involved during the lesson?	• Ten students said yes and provided examples of activities the teacher has used. • Twenty students said no and that they have drifted off regularly in class. • The remaining students said there are times when they have been engaged and other times when they have become disengaged.

Figure 6.7: Sample summary of student feedback trends.

Because descriptive, qualitative information can require more interpretation, you'll want to be sure to involve the teacher in open discussions about the data, what it might mean, and how he or she can use this information in his or her classroom. Following are some steps to guide these discussions once the data have been collected and reviewed.

▸ Have the teacher share his or her general impressions of the student classroom feedback data that were gathered.

▸ Have the teacher identify the trends he or she anticipated and those not anticipated. Ask the teacher to share his or her reactions to this information.

▸ Ask the teacher to share what he or she learned and how he or she plans to implement this learning in future teaching.

▸ Ask the teacher to share how he or she thinks the student feedback could be used in the summative evaluation. Share your thoughts on the possible use of this information in the summative evaluation.

▸ Thank the teacher for implementing a process for gathering student classroom feedback and for discussing what he or she learned in the process.

A Look Back

Earlier in this chapter, we introduced you to Robert, who was working with his principal, Erin, to gather data reflecting students' feedback related to his classroom. Robert received good feedback about how his class was organized from the survey.

Robert and Erin worked together to complete Robert's summative evaluation report. Earlier in the year, Erin had observed Robert effectively managing his classroom but was only able to provide observational feedback. Now that the student feedback provided more details, she was able to make an even stronger case for her analysis of his teaching strengths. The two decided to combine the data from her observations with the data from the surveys. This helped Robert see which strategies were most effective in his classroom management and provided documentation of exceptional performance for his performance evaluation. Erin said that she would like Robert to consider sharing some of his ideas and strategies at a workshop with the other teachers. Robert said he would be interested in sharing some ideas with his colleagues.

Because both the observational data and the student feedback were in agreement, Erin and Robert concluded that classroom management was an area of strength for Robert. In some cases, the supervisor and the principal will want to include more than just two data sources in their conversation, and when data sources are not in agreement, it is necessary for the parties to discuss these differences and further analyze the data. The exact data sources and the number under consideration depend on the exact situation, but examining the situation from multiple perspectives helps the supervisor and the teacher discuss the situation and the adjustments the teacher will be required to make.

Chapter Summary

In this chapter, we discussed ways to gather and use student feedback about classroom conditions in the teacher evaluation and professional growth process. While many teachers are not accustomed to using this type of alternative data, they can provide very helpful insights for teachers.

As you reflect on the information you learned in this chapter, respond to the following questions.

▶ What are the various ways you can gather student feedback related to the classroom?

▶ How can you involve the teacher in analyzing student classroom feedback information?

▶ What are some considerations that need to be taken into account before implementing student classroom feedback as a part of the teacher evaluation process?

Now that you have had an opportunity to learn more about using portfolios and student classroom feedback, we hope you'll take advantage of these resources to work with teachers more effectively. When you first start these processes, teachers may express that they are uncomfortable with them, but if you use them in a positive and professional manner, teachers will become accustomed to them and even value the information they provide.

In the next chapter, we will examine using another alternative data source in the evaluation process—student achievement data.

chapter 7

Using Student Achievement Data

Fred, a middle school mathematics teacher, was preparing for a meeting with his principal, Sheri. The most recent state testing results had just arrived, and about 30 percent of Fred's students did not pass the seventh-grade test. Fred was a little worried about what was going to happen in this meeting. For the meeting, Sheri had invited the mathematics coach, Jennifer, to attend. Fred, Jennifer, and Sheri talked about the situation and determined that one of the problems causing the low performance on the test was the students' lack of understanding of basic mathematical concepts. Together, they developed a plan in which Fred would work with this small group on a weekly basis, the students would be required to participate in an after-school mathematics program, and Jennifer would visit Fred's classroom weekly to coach him in working with these students.

After Jennifer left the meeting, Fred and Sheri continued to talk about the testing situation. Sheri shared with Fred that while test results accounted for only a portion of his performance evaluation, it was a crucial aspect he needed to address. She said that improving his students' mathematics performance would be a major part of his professional growth goals for the upcoming year. Together, they developed a plan integrating the coaching he would receive from Jennifer, some changes he was making in his teaching, and ways to improve his students' understanding of basic mathematics concepts. The plan also included follow-up meetings, observations, and the administration of periodic assessments to measure student progress in the basic mathematics processes.

In this scenario, since the achievement issue was recent, Sheri wisely used the professional planning process to begin to address the situation rather than discipline or threaten Fred. Approaching it this way allowed her to work with Fred in a *supervisory* manner, using the student achievement data as one piece of the picture. Obviously, if the situation does not improve, Sheri will need to decide if she has to take some further action based on her *evaluation* of Fred's performance. Sheri will need to look at Fred's entire performance (including his teaching skills, planning skills, and assessment skills) when determining the next steps.

Chapter Focus

In this chapter, we will focus on student achievement data as a part of the supervision and evaluation process. As you read the information contained in this chapter, you will learn the following.

▸ Common sources of student achievement data and the information they can provide

▸ Considerations to keep in mind when using student achievement data in the supervision and evaluation processes

▸ Strategies for collaborating with the teacher when integrating student achievement sources into the evaluation process

▸ Factors to consider when dealing with student data concerns, including understanding the relationship between student achievement and other aspects of the teacher's performance

Student achievement data have been used for a number of years in the school improvement process. Principals have worked with PLCs, grade-level groups, and other teams in developing school and team plans for using data. The use of these types of data has become a part of many new state evaluation processes for evaluating individual teachers.

Common Sources of Student Achievement Data

There are many types of student achievement data available for use in the teacher supervision and evaluation process. Potential student achievement data sources include the following.

▸ **State testing information:** State achievement testing can provide a good source of information related to student achievement. However, it can also be problematic because there may be gaps in the content areas and grade levels tested.

▶ **Standardized testing:** While some standardized tests do not always reflect local challenges and learning priorities, they do reflect some broad content and learning process outcomes. Some standardized tests include comprehensive items and topical analysis. This level of analysis can provide a focus for individual teachers or collaborative teams.

▶ **Advanced Placement (AP) testing:** While AP tests assess student content mastery, they also provide important information that can be specifically matched to a teacher, class, or program. Using this type of student achievement data over several years may help you identify trends in teaching and learning.

▶ **College placement testing:** While college placement testing such as ACT or SAT tests are designed to measure individual student performance, this information can help identify trends over time. Some schools in the United States have aligned their curricula to these tests. In those cases, the results over time may be helpful in the supervision of teachers.

▶ **Locally developed assessments:** Since state tests only measure student achievement at a point in time, locally developed assessments can provide periodic measures of student learning. Locally developed assessments may be more closely aligned to the district curriculum and priorities. These assessments can be administered multiple times during a year or evaluation cycle, which may help an administrator work with a teacher in a coaching situation.

▶ **Unit or chapter tests:** Unit or chapter assessments provide even more opportunities for periodic use during the school year or evaluation cycle. They hold the potential to be even more focused on the unique or specialized curricula being implemented in the district. However, unit or chapter tests do present some difficulties. Since they are typically designed by the teacher, there may be biases, design flaws, and so on. It may be hard to get accurate assessment data since the teacher gathered them. Even with these difficulties, unit or chapter tests can be a good source of data.

▶ **Quizzes:** Quizzes provide an opportunity to look at student achievement on an even more regular basis. However, they do present difficulties similar to those of unit or chapter tests.

▶ **Student work products and projects:** Because student work products and projects give us an ongoing picture of students' knowledge, they can help educators examine regular trends in student learning. When using student products and projects to assess teachers and student learning, keep in mind that they are subject to the biases of the teachers.

▸ **Exit cards and learning demonstrations:** Some teachers gather almost daily information about how their students are performing. At the end of a class, a teacher may use an exit card to have the students show their learning. An exit card can take many forms, but they are typically demonstrations of learning like a sample problem or sentence. Students show the teacher the completed exit card or required learning demonstration as they leave the classroom at the end of class. Teachers can collect these to show the level of student learning.

As you can see, these student achievement data sources each have strengths and limitations. The supervisor and the teacher should work together to identify which data sources can provide the most accurate information and help the supervisor and the teacher determine the best areas for professional growth.

Considerations When Using Student Achievement Data

Taking into account all of the issues surrounding using student achievement scores to evaluate teachers, we recommend the following.

▸ In several states, the use of student achievement data is mandated by law. Be sure to follow your state's mandates.

▸ Keep in mind that student achievement data are one source of information. There are many other data sources that can help measure a teacher's performance.

▸ Do not make employment decisions solely on student achievement data. These data may not tell the entire story of a teacher's performance. Student achievement data may be impacted by changes in classroom makeup, changing demographics, more complex learning objectives, and a variety of other factors. Thus, basing employment decisions (such as retention, contract status, placing teachers in intensive assistance programs, and so on) solely on student achievement data could be problematic and unfair to the teacher.

▶ Since the use of student achievement data has been focused on school, grade level, subject area, and other broad-based group use, move with caution when using it for individual teachers. Consider reflecting on student achievement data within the context of PLC goals, grade-level goals, and even the teacher's professional growth goals. For example, consider a grade-level collaborative team focusing on improving student achievement in writing. When the standardized tests results come in, the supervisor and the teachers hold a discussion about the test results and the PLC goal. The improved test results show some progress toward the PLC goal. The conversation between the supervisor and teacher reflects this partial progress, and the two decide that even though the goal was not completely achieved, adequate progress was still made toward the goal. In another example, the student achievement test results do not show much growth, but the teacher has gathered informal achievement data using unit assessments and student work samples. These more informal achievement sources show that the students are making good gains. The supervisor and the teacher decide that the achievement is on track and plan to continue to implement the same strategies.

▶ Consider using student data as sources to confirm other data sources. For example, if you have concerns about a teacher's observed performance, you can examine the learning of the students. If the achievement data show that the students are performing poorly, you could include those data when making a decision about working to improve the teacher's performance. Consider using a coaching approach first when dealing with student achievement issues. Talking with a teacher, trying to understand what's happening in the classroom, and developing a plan can let the teacher know you are interested in helping him or her overcome an issue versus "catching" him or her in a problematic situation.

As you work with your teachers, you may want to consider other options, as long as they fit the requirements of your district.

Strategies for Collaborating With the Teacher

Obviously, it's desirable to work with the teacher if possible when using student data as a part of the supervision and evaluation process. To use student achievement data in a collaborative manner with a teacher, discuss their use during a planning conference and integrate them into the professional growth process.

A student achievement data planning conference should have a clear agenda and purpose. Figure 7.1 provides an example of a completed planning form for use in this type of conference.

Use the following form to plan the specific focus of your student achievement data. In your planning, consider strategies you might integrate into your professional growth goals.

Name: _Fred Smith_   Subject or grade level: _Geometry_

Evaluator: _Sheri Banda_   Date: _September 14_

Student achievement data focus (circle all that apply):

  State testing data

  Standardized testing data

  AP testing data

  College placement testing data

  ⟨Unit or chapter testing data⟩

  Local assessment data

  Quizzes

  ⟨Student work products and projects⟩

  Exit cards and other informal assessment data

Student Achievement Data Area	Learning Goal for Data Analysis
Unit or chapter testing data	See how students perform in several units where new teaching strategies are being implemented.
Student work products and projects	Examine the connection between daily performance and unit performance.

Dates for follow-up meetings to discuss the trends and learning based on the data:

September 28

October 17

Figure 7.1: Sample student achievement data use planning form.

*Visit **go.solution-tree.com/leadership** for a reproducible version of this figure.*

Consider the following steps when working with teachers on how to use student achievement data.

1. Ask the teacher to share the desired focus of his or her data examination process.

2. Have the teacher share the specific outcomes for the data examination process.

3. Have the teacher share some of the details about how he or she plans to gather and examine the student data.

4. Discuss how you plan to work with the teacher to integrate the student achievement data into the broader teacher evaluation process and the summative evaluation. Get the teacher's ideas, and share any thoughts you may have about this aspect of the evaluation process.

5. Have the teacher share how he or she plans to keep you updated on the examination of the student achievement data. Identify any follow-up meetings you plan to hold.

The steps for ongoing coaching conferences outlined in chapter 3 (page 49) may also be helpful in guiding follow-up conversations about the use of student data.

As you approach the end of the evaluation cycle, hold a meeting to discuss what was accomplished in the process, the teacher's perception of the process, and how the student achievement data should be used as a part of the summative evaluation. The dialogue in this meeting should be collaborative in nature. You'll want to make sure the experience is positive and productive. Consider the following conversation steps as you approach this conference.

1. Have the teacher share his or her general impressions of the data analysis process.

2. Have the teacher identify what went well and areas that didn't go so well during the student achievement data analysis process.

3. Ask the teacher to share what he or she learned in examining student achievement data and how he or she plans to implement this learning in future teaching.

4. Thank the teacher for his or her work on examining student achievement data and for sharing what he or she learned in the process.

In most situations, we want to use student data in our collaborative work with teachers to help them grow professionally. Occasionally, you may encounter situations where student performance is so poor or consistently low that you need to use a more directive approach in working with teachers whose students have persistent achievement problems.

Factors to Consider When Dealing With Student Data Concerns

In situations where student performance data are especially troubling, it will be important to consider the following factors when deciding how to approach your supervision of and work with a teacher.

Characteristics of Different Data Sources

It's important that you understand the strengths, limitations, and unique characteristics of the various student achievement data sources available to you. For example, standardized testing information is normally clear and easy to understand. Standardized achievement tests may have been developed to reflect state standards and may not match local achievement priorities. Localized assessments might be aligned to local student achievement standards but may lack the reliability and validity needed to use it as a sole achievement measure. You will want to think about and discuss the various strengths and limitations before you decide how to use achievement information in the teacher evaluation and growth process. If you understand the unique issues that exist in your chosen data sources, you will be able to determine how to use them when working with your teachers.

Severity of the Problem

When determining your potential course of action with a teacher, you'll want to consider several factors. Do not base your determination of what to do next only on a test score or poor class performance. As you analyze the student achievement data, try to determine how poor the student performance is in relation to the expected performance. In some cases, the curriculum being taught may not match the test being administered, the achievement of the particular class may be lower in general than others, the teacher may not have had an opportunity to make a positive impact on students' growth as learners, or the overall achievement may have been impacted by several extremely low-performing students.

Relationship Between Student Achievement and Other Aspects of the Teacher's Performance

If the student achievement issues match other areas where you see the teacher as marginal or deficient, you may want to take further action. For example, if the testing data show student deficiencies in content knowledge, and if you have observed that the teacher is not doing a good job teaching the content, you'll want to consider taking some action with the teacher. If other areas of the teacher's performance don't seem to align with the student achievement issues, you may want to study the situation in more depth to determine the cause of the issue.

Understanding the relationship between the performance areas and the student achievement data is crucial for your efforts to either measure the teaching performance (evaluate) or help the teacher improve (supervise). In a case where you are evaluating the performance of the teacher and possibly moving toward contract termination, you'll want to gather data in other performance areas to document poor teaching performance. In a case where you are trying to help the teacher improve, you will want to provide coaching, growth opportunities, feedback, and so on.

Conferences

When addressing performance concerns, it's crucial to start with a verbal notice to the teacher, in the form of a conference. See chapter 8 (page 119) for a comprehensive discussion of the conferencing process, and refer to the "Conferencing Template for Working With Student Achievement Concerns" in appendix B (pages 193–194) for a specific template to guide your conversation with the teacher about student achievement data concerns. Feel free to adapt this template based on your own unique needs or situation.

A Look Back

In the middle of the school year, Sheri scheduled a meeting with Fred to see how his improvement efforts were going. In the meeting, she shared feedback from some of the walkthrough visits she had made to his classroom. She said she noticed that Fred was presenting his content in a clearer and more concise manner and that he was getting the students more engaged in processing the learning objectives. Fred had also aligned his content units to better match the sequencing for the testing. He had formatted some of his assignments and practice opportunities to match the ways students would be asked to respond on the test. Finally, he had worked with his mathematics coach, Jennifer, to develop some strategies to use in his classroom to help prepare his students for the test. Fred specifically added the use of informal achievement data sources like exit cards and student work samples. He noticed that he was able to immediately see which students understood and did not understand the learning objectives in his classes. Fred and Sheri felt positive about his progress and knew that his efforts would pay off by increasing the students' achievement on the upcoming assessments.

In this example, we see how Fred and Sheri worked together to use the student achievement information (test data) as a part of the plan for Fred's improvement. While Sheri was concerned about student achievement, she worked with Fred to set a course and align resources to help him move toward being successful. He may not completely solve the issue in one year but is now on track to improve both his teaching and the students' achievement over time. She worked with Fred, not against him, to help him understand what needed to be changed and how to move forward. This stance helps reduce the resistance principals sometimes get when working with teachers. It also helps the teacher see that there are multiple facets to the issue and allows the teacher to work collaboratively and constructively to improve student achievement.

Chapter Summary

In this chapter, we discussed using student achievement data in the teacher evaluation and growth process. While student achievement data have been used in the past for school or team goals, they have not been widely used in measuring individual teacher performance. However, they may be required in new teacher evaluation processes. Using these data in a collaborative or proactive manner with a teacher is optimal because the supervisor and the teacher are working together to integrate student achievement data into the supervision and evaluation process.

As you reflect on the information you learned in this chapter, respond to the following questions.

▸ Why is it important to focus on the use of student achievement data in a collaborative manner? What strategies can you use to work collaboratively with your teachers, using student data to evaluate and improve teacher performance?

▸ What are the major types of student data available for use in the supervision and evaluation process? What are the strengths and limitations for each type?

‣ When should student achievement and observational concerns be tied together? Why is it important to include classroom observational data with student achievement data in deciding how to work with teachers when student achievement concerns emerge?

While we have touched on the need for conferencing briefly in this chapter, in the next chapter you will learn some foundational ideas about conducting conferences with teachers. These will be helpful as you work to implement the requirements of your teacher evaluation process.

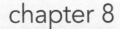

chapter 8

Conferencing With Teachers

Cassandra was the new principal at Delvin Middle School. She had been conducting classroom visits for the past month. One of her latest observations was in a science classroom. Bill was an outspoken veteran teacher. While reviewing her classroom observation notes, Cassandra identified some areas of concern that she wanted to discuss with Bill; for instance, he seemed to be using some outdated strategies. How would she go about bringing up these concerns while still maintaining the relationship that she had begun to build with Bill? How would he take her ideas and suggestions? Cassandra thought through her conference plan carefully, focusing on how to best approach the situation with Bill.

Cassandra decided she would approach the situation by focusing on Bill's past history and teaching accomplishments. She approached this conference differently than her last conference because she thought that Bill could benefit from coupling his past successes with new ideas for growth. She would build on his commitment and accomplishments to help him learn new strategies to better teach his students. She carefully scripted what she was going to say during each phase of the instructional conference she would have with Bill.

In the conference, Cassandra asked Bill to reflect on some of the areas he thought went well and others that didn't go as he had expected. Bill shared his perceptions and, in response to Cassandra's clear questions, brought up one of the areas that Cassandra noticed as a concern. Bill said he appreciated the fact that Cassandra asked him for his reflections before she shared her thoughts. He said this gave him the opportunity to think and develop his own ideas.

After Bill was finished with his analysis, Cassandra confirmed his positive attributes and then began to explain some ideas that would help Bill address his areas of concern. Bill listened carefully, making notes as Cassandra spoke. Cassandra shared several strategies for how they might work together to incorporate these new ideas into Bill's teaching.

At the end of the conference, Bill thanked Cassandra for sharing the new ideas with him. He said this was the first time in his career that a principal was able to sit down and explain how to implement new ideas in his classroom. He found the entire experience very helpful.

Does this situation sound too good to be true? Did Cassandra give Bill a drink of some magic potion before this conference? How was she so successful in helping a veteran teacher like Bill examine his teaching and be receptive to new ideas?

The outcome in this example is based on the professional relationship Cassandra worked to develop with Bill and her use of an informative, instructional conference. Rather than just tell Bill what to do, Cassandra actually tailored her conference to fit the way Bill processes information. She also planned the conference so that it would be an instructional experience for Bill. Cassandra modeled the same sort of skill she was asking all of her teachers to perform—using instructionally sound explanations.

Chapter Focus

Masterful supervision conferences can go a long way in helping teachers learn and grow and helping supervisors model the instructional strategies they would like their teachers to use with their students. In this chapter, we will examine the supervision strategy of using instructionally based conferences to help teachers grow. More specifically, we will discuss the following.

▶ The need for feedback and learning opportunities

▶ Reasons supervisors should use conferences, including to maintain effective practices and improve current methods

▶ A conferencing template you can use to communicate concerns with teachers

▶ Suggestions to guide conferences addressing poor performance

The Need for Feedback

As school leaders, we work in a learning environment. While the teachers we work with are responsible for student learning, we are responsible for teacher learning. In order for our students to learn effectively, we have to provide opportunities for teachers to learn. Author Margaret Wheatley (1992) discusses the importance of congruency in organizations. Her work shows us that leaders can't just tell people what to do and expect them to follow through; instead, they should provide the same types of learning experiences for teachers that they want students to have in the classroom. For example, if a supervisor wants the teachers to work with their students in a developmental nature, this supervisor should provide the same types of learning opportunities for the teachers in the school. In Wheatley's opinion, we have to model what we want our teachers to do in their classrooms.

This principle is very important in the work supervisors do in schools. One way supervisors can make a huge difference in the learning of their teachers is through the supervision process. This process should provide employees with information that helps them continue to maintain their effective skills and also refine areas of their teaching to keep their practices current. Unfortunately, we have found that in many schools, the supervision and evaluation aspects of the job have been reduced to checklists, email notices, or even processes in which teachers receive no feedback. However, Daniel Goleman, Richard Boyatzis, and Annie McKee (2002) contend that, in an environment absent of feedback, employees tend to think they're doing well and do not need to make any changes.

Reasons Supervisors Should Use Conferences

Supervisors can provide the learning that teachers need through the use of instructional conferences. The prime focus of these conferences is on learning rather than cutting a staff member down, reprimanding a behavior, or calling the teacher out. There are times when a supervisor needs to conduct a difficult conference, but most supervisory conferences should include some type of learning for the teacher.

When thinking about implementing instructional conferences, it is important to decide what type of information might be most helpful to the teacher participating in the conference. Additionally, consider the kind of learning opportunities the teacher needs to experience in the instructional conference. Some teachers might need an opportunity to think and reflect on their instruction, while others need you to provide information and act as another pair of eyes for them.

Just as supervisors expect their teachers to have clear learning outcomes, objectives, and instructional strategies in mind when they teach, supervisors should do the same when they construct instructional conferences. For example, if a supervisor wants an effective teacher to understand what's making his or her instruction effective and then be able to maintain these effective practices, the supervisor should conference with the teacher to help him or her see how this is done. If a supervisor wants a teacher to understand what is working well in his or her instruction and then refine or expand his or her teaching skills, this supervisor needs to provide these opportunities in a conference. Finally, if a supervisor wants a teacher to understand why some of his strategies are not working and to have a chance to develop ways of refining his teaching, an instructional conference will assist the teacher in achieving this objective. An instructional conference is designed to help a teacher learn what is effective so she can continue to perform well in those areas while also learning what could be improved or refined to make her teaching even better in the future.

Conferencing Template

When planning and delivering instructional conferences for teachers, the process should occur in three distinct learning phases: (1) providing a focus for the conference, (2) helping the teacher learn about the teaching performance, and (3) ensuring the major recommendations from the conference are applied in the classroom. Each phase contains a number of instructional conference components designed to fit together to provide a smooth conferencing experience. These phases and components are outlined in the following sections and include sample statements you may want to use during the conference.

Conferencing Phase I: Providing a Focus for the Conference

To focus the conference, the supervisor must first set the proper tone by letting the teacher know that the conference will be a professional experience. Sample statements include:

> ▶ "Thank you for coming in today to talk about your teaching. It's nice to have people like you who are dedicated to students working here. I know that your time is valuable, so I'll stay focused during this conference today."

- ▸ "Thank you for meeting with me today and talking about this professionally important topic."

- ▸ "Thanks for your willingness to get together and talk about your teaching."

All of these statements communicate to the teacher that the upcoming instructional conference will be a learning experience. Setting a professional tone helps the teacher focus and learn during the instructional conference experience. If a professional tone is not set at the beginning of a conference, the supervisor and the teacher may not approach the experience with the same expectations, and the supervisor runs the risk that the instructional conference may erode to just a conversation or a rating of skills.

Next, the supervisor needs to provide an overview or outline for the instructional conference. It helps to establish the agenda and objective by letting the teacher know what to expect. Use this phase of the conference to lay out the plan for your time with the teacher. Sample statements include:

- ▸ "During this conference, I plan to ask you for your perception of the lesson—what you think went well and what you would change if you were to teach it again. Then I'll give you my perceptions of the effective areas and those that may need refinement. Finally, we'll explore how we can work together to continue to hone your teaching skills."

- ▸ "As we work together today to address the issue, we will use the following format—

  - ▸ "I'll share my observations of the level of student engagement in your classroom."

  - ▸ "I'll give you a chance to provide your perspectives on how you felt the lesson went."

  - ▸ "We'll talk about how I can support you as you continue to implement new assessment ideas to gain more knowledge about the learning needs of your students."

Providing an overview for the experience also helps draw parameters around the topics of conversation in the instructional conference. For example, if a supervisor starts out the instructional conference by saying, "Today, I'll provide you with feedback about your student engagement efforts, then we will explore strategies together to help strengthen this area of your teaching," then the agenda for the meeting is already set. If the teacher tries to bring up excuses related to why he can't improve the level of achievement, the supervisor can redirect the conference back to the stated topic.

Conferencing Phase II: Helping the Teacher Learn About the Teaching Performance

During the second phase, the supervisor asks the teacher questions to help him or her reflect on the event and share his or her perceptions. By asking for the teacher's perceptions, the supervisor works to build the teacher's observational or reflective skills. The supervisor can also share his or her perceptions about the teaching performance, which can be helpful if the supervisor believes that the teacher is unable to provide a perspective on the lesson or wants to avoid putting the teacher on the spot to come up with reflections. Another factor that supervisors may consider including when giving their feedback is the accuracy of the teacher's perception of the lesson. Sometimes people may think that the lesson was great when it was not. Don't just accept a teacher's perception if you think much differently than he or she does about the lesson. Sample statements include:

▸ "As you think back to the lesson, how do you think things went overall? What went well? What didn't go as planned?"

▸ "From your perspective, what went well and what didn't go well in this lesson?"

▸ "As you think about your performance this year, talk about your areas of growth, and then share areas that continue to challenge you."

Next, the evaluator should provide specific feedback, including examples of effective teaching practices. In this section, you can give the teacher feedback about the lesson and what worked or went well from your perspective. Sample statements include:

▸ "As I watched the lesson, I noticed that _____ really seemed to be working well for you. That is an example of _____ from the teaching performance standards the district has adopted. Since it is effective, you should continue to use it in the future." (Up to three or four effective areas can be mentioned.)

▸ "In my observations, I've been able to see some positive trends in your teaching. Let me share a few of them here."

▸ "While there are many areas where you are doing a good job, three teaching areas stand out above the others. Let me share specific examples of when I've seen these used in your classroom, and the impact I observed on the students in your classes."

Then, the evaluator tells the teacher what needs to be changed in his or her future teaching performance. This section of the conference is where you can thoroughly explain or teach something the teacher needs to improve or refine. Sample statements include:

- ▸ "One area that was not quite as effective as it could be was _____. Let me explain what this principle is all about. [*Explains.*] In the future, it is my expectation that you include this in your instruction to the students."

- ▸ "I've noticed in the last few walkthrough observations I've conducted that you have been _____. This area is still coming together for you. Let me share some strategies."

Conferencing Phase III: Ensuring the Major Recommendations From the Conference Are Applied in the Classroom

In the third phase, the supervisor begins by asking questions to make sure the teacher understands the marginal area and what his or her expectations are for the needed improvement. Ensuring that the teacher understands the issue and what improvements are expected is key to success. Asking clarifying questions can feel unnatural, but it ensures the expectations are clear. Now, if the performance does not improve, the supervisor can move forward in taking additional actions because he or she can be sure the teacher understood what needed to be changed. Sample questions to check the teacher's understanding include:

- ▸ "I want to make sure you are successful in changing _____. What are my expectations, and when do I want you to be implementing them?"

- ▸ "If you were going to share the major points of our discussion with _____, what would they be?"

- ▸ "This conversation was very productive and regards something very important for your future here at _____. What's your understanding of my expectations regarding your behavior?"

- ▸ "Before we leave, let's take a minute to review what was discussed and what we agreed on as a result of our time together today."

Finally, the supervisor shares the plan for follow-up to ensure the recommended changes are made in the classroom. Follow-up is essential to the success of any teacher evaluation process. Here the supervisor clearly communicates the plan to check in with the teacher in the future to make sure that the refinement area shared during the instructional conference is being implemented. Sample statements include:

- "We both agree that _____ is an important area for you to use in your teaching. I'll stop back in a couple of weeks to see how you are integrating it into your teaching."
- "Now that we both are on the same page, I plan to come to your classroom next week to see you _____."
- "In order to support you through this change, I plan to stop by next week to talk with you about how you have _____."
- "As you develop _____, you need to send them to me so I can review them before _____."

Conferences Addressing Poor Performance

It is sometimes necessary to conduct conferences that are not as routine and are more serious in nature. Teachers whose performance is considered marginal or deficient will require a slightly different type of conference to address these problems. We outline the aspects for conferencing with deficient teachers in this section. Chapter 9 (page 131) provides more detailed information about working with these teachers.

When conducting conferences with teachers who are deficient in their performance, it's important to stay focused and on track. The conference itself needs to be clear and address your concerns. It's also important to tell the teacher that his or her performance is well below expectations and that you have serious concerns about his or her teaching. As you get closer to the end of the termination process, you will also want to let the teacher know that you are considering recommending that his or her contract not be renewed or terminated. The following list, adapted from Eller and Eller (2010), provides an outline for clearly communicating issues and concerns while setting expectations for change.

- **Set a professional tone:** At the beginning of the conference, you'll want to set a professional tone. This will be important because it will help keep the conversation on track. Setting a professional tone should be done through a statement made by the supervisor at the beginning of the conference. Examples of statements are listed in the "Sample Statement Starters for Deficient Teacher or Termination Conversations" form in appendix B (pages 195–197).

▶ **Provide an overview of the agenda for the conference:** By providing an overview of the conference agenda, you frame the conversation. This framing draws a boundary around the conversation and helps keep it on track during the conference.

▶ **Define the missing or deficient skill:** It's important that you clearly identify the issue or problem. In this section of the conference, you need to let the teacher know the exact issues you have with his or her performance by stating them clearly and not skirting around the issue.

▶ **Give clear, clean examples of the deficiency and why it is a deficiency:** In this section of the conference, you need to provide the specific examples of evidence you have gathered reflecting the deficiency area. Providing the evidence minimizes the possibility of disagreement. It's hard to argue with factual information.

▶ **Tell the teacher he or she is not meeting the performance standards:** It might seem obvious, but it's important to tell the teacher that he or she is not meeting the standard or expectations. By clearly stating that the teacher is not meeting the standards, you ensure there is no misinterpretation.

▶ **Define the required skill or level of performance needed in order to meet the standards:** Now that you have told the teacher what is wrong, you need to let him or her know what you expect to happen in order for the teacher to be considered as performing up to expectations. By defining this level of expectations, you help provide a target for the teacher to attain.

▶ **Ask the teacher to share what he or she learned in the conference and what changes need to occur in the classroom:** Now that you have clearly laid out the problem and the expectations, you need to make sure the teacher understands what was discussed in this conference. By taking the time to check the teacher's understanding, you eliminate the possibility of confusion and increase the level of accountability. Everyone should leave the conference with a clear understanding of the expectations and the next steps in the process.

▶ **Set clear expectations for integration of the new skill into the classroom, including the timeline for implementation:** The end of the conference is a good time to let the teacher know that you plan to follow up on the expectations set in this conference. One good way to do that is to let the teacher know that you plan to stop by to see how he or she is implementing the information discussed in the conference. Clearly communicating your follow-up plan raises accountability but also lets the teacher know that you care and are willing to check in on his or her progress. This is a subtle but important message to communicate at the end of the conference.

It's crucial to develop your talking points or a script for the conference in advance of the meeting. By developing a script, you will have the exact wording that you need to use in the conference. Planned wording is important because these conferences can become emotional, making it is easy to get off track or forget key points. A script will help you stay on track. Visit **go.solution-tree.com/leadership** to access the blank template "Conferencing Template for Working With Deficient Teachers," and consult the form "Sample Statement Starters for Deficient Teacher or Termination Conversations" in appendix B (pages 195–197) for tools to help you plan a conference and develop your script.

A Look Back

Cassandra had worked to develop a clear teaching and learning conference when she met with Bill to share her observations. He told her that the conferences were a positive experience for him and that he learned a lot in the process. Bill looked forward to the conversations he had with Cassandra and how she clearly explained what she saw happening in his classroom. Thus, he came to every conference having given some thought to what happened in the lesson. Soon, he was taking a lead in the conferences and Cassandra was adding her thoughts and details. This was a much different experience for Bill than the "telling" conferences he had experienced in the past.

In this example, you can see how making conferences a learning experience for teachers can help change the perception of the teacher evaluation process in a building. When we help teachers learn, they, in turn, will use these same strategies in the classroom. Many teachers have never experienced supervision conferences where they have been active participants. By setting the expectations for them to come prepared to share their perspectives, we help them bring their ideas to the table and learn in the process.

Keep in mind that there are teachers and situations where you as the supervisor will want to conduct a more directive conference. In situations where a teacher cannot see the issues, or is unwilling to admit them, you may encounter trouble in having him or her take a lead in the conferencing process. Also, in cases where you are working to document deficient or marginal performance, it may be hard for some teachers to see the issues. The set of strategies that we will address in chapter 9 will help in those instances.

Chapter Summary

When working through the evaluation process with teachers, it's important to conduct conferences during which you explain what is effective in their performance and what needs to be changed or refined about their performance. A clear and well-planned conference helps teachers see exactly how their performance measures up against your standards and expectations. Even though we live in an era of short, focused, and electronic communications, feedback about teaching is not an area that should be shortened or reduced. Conducting a high-quality conference shows that you value adult learning and growth. This is the same kind of learning and growth that you want your teachers to provide for their students.

As you reflect on the information you learned in this chapter, respond to the following questions.

▸ What is the rationale behind conducting conferences that promote learning on the part of teachers?

▸ Why would you need to consider using a conference that has phases or stages? What are the goals of the various stages or phases presented in this chapter?

▸ How does asking teachers to share their perceptions of the lesson help them to better utilize the performance feedback you share with them in a conference?

Now that you have a general understanding of the importance of a conference and know how to design and plan a conference, it's time to explore another aspect of evaluating your teachers. In the next chapter, we will examine the process of working productively with marginal and deficient teachers.

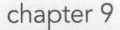

chapter 9

Understanding and Addressing Marginal and Deficient Teachers

Tom, a high school principal, had just completed a walkthrough observation in one of his mathematics teacher's classrooms. His observation confirmed what he had been hearing from parents and students for the last year. Marty, the mathematics teacher, wasn't doing a good job. This wasn't a new situation. Tom had talked with Marty about this situation over the last two years. In addition to the feedback he had been receiving from students and parents, Tom had also noticed that the students in Marty's class were performing below those in other mathematics sections. Tom knew he had to take action but didn't know where he should start. After all, Marty was an outgoing staff member and was very supportive of his leadership.

Encountering teachers who are performing at a low level compared to their peers and the expectations of the school and the district is a situation many supervisors face. In the past, some of these teachers may not have been noticed, but in today's environment of high accountability, they are very visible.

Chapter Focus

In this chapter, we examine some background information regarding marginal and deficient teachers. This information will help you begin the process of either working with teachers to develop and implement strategies to help them improve or considering their termination. So, how can principals work with these teachers to improve their performance? How can principals explain what is wrong with their teaching and provide clear direction about what needs to be changed in order for them to be successful? What do principals need to do if reasonable performance expectations aren't met? In this chapter, you will learn the following.

- ▸ An understanding of the concepts of marginal and deficient teaching performance

- ▸ Types of marginal teachers you may encounter, along with tips for working with them

- ▸ Strategies to help identify marginal teacher types, especially through trends and patterns that show the quality and consistency of the teaching is well below expectations

- ▸ What to consider when addressing a marginal or deficient teacher, including the administration's attitude, the severity of the problem, and the results of previous remediation attempts

- ▸ Skills needed to address marginal or deficient performance

- ▸ Conferencing strategies to address several marginal teacher types

- ▸ Suggestions for tracking teacher performance

Definitions of Marginal and Deficient Performance

Typically, teaching that does not meet expectations is described as *marginal* or *deficient*. The difference in these two terms is the degree to which the teaching performance is below our expectations, with marginal performance being less severe than deficient performance.

Deficient teachers perform well below teaching performance standards in multiple areas or on a constant basis. Because of the depth of problems that deficient teachers can pose, turning their performance around may be more complex than turning around the performance of a marginal teacher. Also, because some deficient teachers may have been performing at this lower level for extended periods of time, it may take much longer to improve their performance. Deficient teachers are candidates for extensive interventions like intensive assistance processes and directive growth plans, as well as disciplinary action or possible contract termination.

Marginal performance, on the other hand, describes performance that is slightly below or occasionally goes below expectations. Marginal teachers can do an acceptable job in some areas yet perform below expectations in others. Such teachers may be able to improve their performance when given time, assistance, and resources. Danielson and McGreal (2000) define marginal teachers as "those who, in the professional judgment of an administrator, are experiencing difficulty in meeting one or more of the district's standards for effective teaching" (p. 116). A key point in their definition is the judgment of the administrator. The building administrator is the person who defines the standard for performance within a building. Thus, the administrator's judgment of teacher performance is the most important aspect that boards and the courts use in determining possible contract termination.

C. Edward Lawrence (2005) describes the marginal teacher as "unable or unwilling to improve his or her teaching performance and thus has a negative impact on the students" (p. 2). A key aspect of Lawrence's definition is the distinction of unable or unwilling. Supervisors face both of these in their work with marginal teachers. If a teacher is unable to perform at an acceptable level, this means the teacher may lack the basic skills to implement effective instructional practices, and a supervisor may be able to provide assistance to help them improve. A supervisor might consider strategies such as carefully explaining the needed changes or having the marginal teacher work with a peer, a mentor, or an instructional coach. In working with unable teachers, supervisors will need to quickly assess whether the teacher has the capacity to learn and implement the desired skill. If the needed improvements are beyond the scope of what the teacher can learn, the supervisor may need to move toward termination of employment.

In contrast, unwillingness to perform at an acceptable level means that the teacher may possess the abilities needed to be effective but is choosing not to implement them. Teachers who are unwilling pose a different challenge and may require a different set of strategies to improve their performance. Supervisors may need to encourage or motivate the teacher or provide a directive for the teacher to improve or eliminate the problem in their performance.

Improving marginal teachers sometimes requires a customized approach based on the conditions and the situations they face. It can be challenging for supervisors to determine the best way to move forward in working with marginal teachers; thus, understanding what type of marginal teacher you are dealing with will help you in your approach.

Types of Marginal Teachers

While several studies and authors discuss marginal teachers, few examine the different types of marginal teachers. One study by Eileen Beverley Kaye (2004) asked teachers to describe the characteristics of their marginal peers. Three major marginal types emerged: (1) those whose performance is based on a general need to learn and grow (they are aware of this need), (2) those who have fallen behind on their teaching skills because of program or student changes (these teachers are also aware of this situation), and (3) those who are marginal but are not aware of their skill deficit (they may actually think they are doing well). This last group of teachers may even have personal ties to or be friends with the principal and have never been told they are falling behind. Their marginal behavior may have been overlooked for years.

After reviewing Kaye's research, we saw a connection between this research and our previous work with difficult and resistant staff. In our book *Working With Difficult and Resistant Staff* (Eller & Eller, 2011), we identified eight types of teachers who can negatively impact the climate and culture of a building. Three of the types identified in that book match the marginal types Kaye (2004) outlines: (1) the Challenged, (2) On-the-Job Retirees, and (3) Resident Experts.

The Challenged

The Challenged are teachers who lack the skills they need in order to implement effective teaching practices (Eller & Eller, 2011). These are people who may not know how to implement strategies, are new to their position, are learning new skills, or are overwhelmed by improvement initiatives. They are aware they are behind but may try to cover up their deficit (Eller & Eller, 2011). Those in the Challenged category need support in learning the desired skills in order to improve their marginal performance.

The category name should not be seen as negative. Many teachers fitting into this category have a good foundation of teaching skills, are conscientious teachers with good personalities, are eager to learn, and take direction very well. Many of the teachers in the Challenged category are still learning how to teach or implement new skills and will become proficient when given time and support.

When working with the Challenged, supervisors should carefully examine the areas in which these teachers are not performing at the expectation level of the building or district. Then, the supervisor will need to assist the teacher in developing a plan that breaks the expectations into attainable parts with a timeline for implementation.

On-the-Job Retirees

On-the-Job Retirees are teachers who have fallen behind on their required teaching skills (Eller & Eller, 2011). These teachers may have a skill set that was effective for older programs or earlier eras of education, but now these skills are no longer meeting the needs of their learners. Some On-the-Job

Retirees are interested in staying current but just don't know how, while others may be interested in just riding out their time at the school. The teachers in this category should be defined by their attitude and behavior, not their age, since they can become On-the-Job Retirees at any age.

When working with On-the-Job Retirees, it's important to try to understand what might be causing this behavior. Some On-the-Job Retirees need support and direction, while others benefit from clear expectations, directives, and follow-up. The On-the-Job Retirees who are conscientious but have just fallen behind can benefit from support that is similar to what might be offered for the Challenged. Other On-the-Job Retirees will need a more direct approach to improve their teaching skills. Some of these strategies include helping them identify their legacy, keeping them engaged and involved in important school activities, providing clear and time-bound directives, or helping them see that their skill set is no longer appropriate and that it might be beneficial for them to seek opportunities outside the field of teaching. The specific strategy chosen to help an On-the-Job Retiree should be based on the teacher's years of experience, informal leadership position within the school, how far below expectations he or she performs, and so on. Above all, On-the-Job Retirees should be treated with respect and dignity.

Resident Experts

Resident Experts act like they know everything but may not be able to implement strategies correctly (Eller & Eller, 2011). Some Resident Experts are aware of their challenges, but others think they are so good that their teaching should be a model. Some may think they are working hard, though you do not see them in the same light. If the performance of Resident Experts has been marginal for an extended period of time, you may need to spend time helping them see that they need to improve. Supervisory conferences need to be direct and regular in order to get the message across.

This category of teachers presents a unique challenge to administrators. Sometimes, the greatest task you may face is helping Resident Experts see that they are not performing up to standards. Obviously, our first choice would be to help them see that they are behind. This task might be accomplished by clearly explaining the difference between their performance and the standards, allowing them to see other teachers in action, providing them with regular and specific feedback, sending them to conferences or providing professional development, and so on. Once they are able to see the problem, you can work with them in a manner similar to how you work with the Challenged. This approach would involve breaking the expectations into parts and asking them to improve their performance based on stages and a clear timeline.

In other cases, Resident Experts are not going to see or buy in to the fact that their teaching is below standard. In these cases, no amount of convincing will help them. If you're waiting for these teachers to get on board, you might be waiting several years. If you've repeatedly been unsuccessful in using the methods we've listed here to convince a Resident Expert that his or her teaching is marginal, it's time to move to a new strategy. For this situation, you should consider using your positional power as this teacher's supervisor or evaluator and provide clear directives and timelines for changing his or her marginal performance.

When you become more directive, don't expect the Resident Expert to agree with you or enjoy the supervision process. Many of the supervisors we have worked with over the years have allowed lack of enthusiasm or buy-in to keep them from addressing marginal teaching behaviors. If you understand up front that your work with this teacher will cause controversy and be met with resistance, you can expect and prepare for this lack of enthusiasm. This discord is one of the most difficult aspects of addressing marginal teaching behavior and one that can cause great emotional stress for the principal. Later, we will discuss how to stay on track when working with these teachers and how to deal with the negative climate these teachers can cause, but first we must learn to identify these categories of teachers.

Identification of Marginal Teacher Types

Being able to identify the types of marginal teachers will help you develop plans and strategies to address their marginal performance. In order to categorize a marginal teacher, you will want to spend a little time assessing and understanding the issue with their performance. The following guide (table 9.1) will help you diagnose the predominant type of marginal teacher you are dealing with.

Keep in mind that some teachers may exhibit multiple performance issues and may not fit neatly into one of these categories. In those cases, identify the dominant marginal teacher type and start by focusing on strategies designed to more productively work with this teacher based on his or her needs. Before tackling the issues of marginal performers, it's important for you to consider several factors, described in the next section.

Table 9.1: Guide for Determining the Primary Type of Marginal Teacher

	The Challenged	On-the-Job Retiree	Resident Expert
General Marginal Issues	Appears to be lacking in knowledge of effective teaching strategies or is unable to implement effective teaching strategies	Appears to be behind the times in knowledge or implementation of general strategies	Appears to be unaware of issues or holds an inflated opinion of self
Teacher's Typical Response When You Address the Concern	Accepts suggestions; seems interested in learning; may ask clarification questions	Does not appear to be interested in suggestions; may put blame on the students or changing times	Openly discounts ideas and suggestions; may become defensive or try to justify existing behaviors; may remind you of how good they are
Results or Impact of Your Improvement Efforts	Gradual or measurable improvements might be made; these improvements may lack fluidity but illustrate some progress	Inconsistent or poor skill application; may appear to be overwhelmed or physically or emotionally taxed in relation to the job performance	May seem to understand when in your presence but has difficulty implementing alone; may try to avoid having you follow up to observe integration of new strategies and skills

Considerations When Addressing a Marginal or Deficient Teacher

In *Working With Difficult and Resistant Staff* (Eller & Eller, 2011), we provide a list of characteristics that administrators can use to decide whether a teacher is marginal or deficient. We have modified that work here to help you think through the implications or ripple effects of addressing the performance of marginal and deficient teachers. The following sections will help you anticipate potential issues you may encounter before moving forward to confront marginal teaching performance or contract termination of a deficient teacher.

The Type of Marginal Teacher

Knowing the type of marginal teacher will help you decide how to address the performance issue. For example, with a Challenged teacher, you may want to approach the situation in an instructional manner, providing opportunities to learn and practice the new strategies. For an On-the-Job-Retiree, you may want to appeal to the teacher's professionalism or past positive reputation. For a Resident Expert, you may need to spend time helping the teacher to see that there is an issue or rely on your positional power to direct the needed changes.

Employment Status

Most states have employment laws governing teacher contract provisions. Because of the legal implications, it's especially important to be aware of the contract status of marginal and deficient teachers when planning to address their performance issues. As discussed in chapter 1, probationary teachers are more easily terminated, whereas continuing contract teachers have already been deemed competent, meaning more responsibility falls on the administrator to bring the teacher's performance up to standards.

Administration or Board's Attitude Toward Addressing Poor Teaching

You should assess the readiness of your superintendent, school board, and community when addressing marginal teaching performance. If one of these entities is not comfortable in moving the process forward, you will not have the support you need during this crucial process. For example, if the superintendent is not in favor of addressing the situation, he or she may not make the necessary recommendations to the board, work with the teachers' union or association, or provide you with the resources or support necessary to improve the marginal teaching. The same is true when considering termination of a deficient teacher.

When you have a situation that may end in a recommendation for termination, immediately notify your superintendent or direct supervisor. Schedule a conference to discuss the situation and the evidence you have to make your case. Since the school board is the body that actually hires and fires employees, your superintendent may need to discuss the situation privately with the board chair and other board members.

Severity of the Teaching Problems

In examining teaching performance, it's crucial to determine how poor the teaching performance is compared to the expectations. A marginal performance would be at least slightly below the performance expectations. If the performance is considerably below expectations, the teacher could be deficient, and more drastic improvement or contract termination strategies should be considered.

Number of Teaching Problem Areas

If a teacher is considered to be marginal, his or her poor performance is normally confined to a few areas of the district's performance expectations. If there are several areas in which a teacher is performing well below expectations, the teacher might be considered deficient. In many cases, the areas of concern are closely related. For example, if a teacher has classroom management issues, he or she may also have issues related to student relationships, curriculum management, student assessment, and so on. This makes your job of finding problems easier but your job of providing any positive feedback more difficult.

In these situations, it may help to find areas of strength and build on them or make generalized encouraging statements like, "I appreciate how you are still trying to implement my recommendations even though the classroom climate is not getting much better," or "You have done a good job implementing the first part of your classroom management plan, but you still have a long way to go before this area is up to the district's standards." However, it's important for supervisors to be open and honest with teachers and let them know that because of the high number of concerns, they will be focusing on improvement rather than providing a lot of positive feedback. Even though these statements don't sound very positive, sincere feedback is better than empty positive feedback that does not contribute to improving the issues at hand.

Specific Areas of Concern

While all areas in the core teaching framework are important, certain behaviors have a more direct impact on students and their achievement. You should prioritize a smaller set of these crucial expectations and make sure the performance in these areas is meeting the standards. For example, in most schools, teachers who develop positive relationships with students have a greater impact on their achievement than those who don't develop these relationships. Meeting this standard might be more important to student success than teachers participating on building-level committees. If you identify a teacher with marginal or deficient performance in the area of student relationships, you may need to act quickly. If you notice a teacher who is lacking in committee involvement, you may address the issue more slowly.

The examples provided here are only for illustration. The exact prioritization of teaching skills should be based on your judgment and the needs of your students and school.

The Relationship Between the Areas of Concern

Another factor supervisors should take into consideration is the relationship between the areas of concern. Some areas have an independent relationship, meaning they can stand alone. Others have a dependent relationship, meaning one depends on another. Finally, some areas are interdependently related, meaning they work together equally in helping students learn.

Understanding the relationship between the performance areas is an important consideration in moving forward with a marginal teacher because it can help supervisors be more successful in improving the marginal performance. For example, if a supervisor notices that a teacher has difficulty with classroom management, and this issue is undermined by a lack of good student relationships, the supervisor may decide to address the teacher-student relationship issue first. Effective classroom management is dependent on good teacher-student relationships, so the supervisor may be wasting her time focusing on management until the relationship issue is addressed. In another situation, a supervisor might notice that a teacher has poorly developed assessments. Upon further examination, this supervisor might find that the assessments are poorly developed because the teacher lacks the content knowledge needed to break down the learning into component parts. The supervisor might decide that content knowledge needs to be coupled with the assessment-development strategies for the teacher to improve the performance because these two areas are interdependent.

Type of Competency in Question

In *Working With and Evaluating Difficult School Employees* (Eller & Eller, 2010), we introduce the concept of base and surface competencies. Base competencies are "the kinds of skills that are at the core of an employee's person or personality. Base competencies cannot be easily taught but must be developed over time with support and coaching" (p. 14). Surface competencies are:

> the kind of skills that are most directly related to the technical aspects of the job. Surface competencies are the skills typically taught to employees as a part of their job orientation/induction process and can be learned fairly quickly and can be measured in a straightforward manner. (p. 15)

Understanding the nature of the skills in question will help you determine the strategies you should employ when working with a particular teacher to improve performance. For example, if a teacher is marginal in breaking a concept into parts (a surface competency) when teaching a lesson, it may be helpful to provide a model of the needed change that could be duplicated in the teacher's classroom.

On the other hand, a teacher who has trouble communicating with parents (a base competency, because the teacher should understand the informational needs of parents by using understanding or empathy) may require more support and time to actually see the issue. This will lengthen the time needed to improve the marginal performance.

Keep in mind that some base competency behaviors may be based on the teacher's personality and may be extremely difficult to change. Understanding the challenges of remediating base competency behaviors may help you determine whether to continue your remediation work or move the teacher to a disciplinary or termination track.

Results of Previous Remediation Attempts

If the teacher is new to the school or field or new to the position, you might give him or her more time to learn and implement the recommended changes. In some cases, marginal skills may have been in place for a number of years and may have been addressed in the past. As this teacher's supervisor, you need to be able to judge the progress the employee has made in relation to the issue, and then determine if that progress is appropriate.

It is also important for you to think about the interventions you have provided in the past and whether they have been appropriate based on the needed improvements. For example, if you have provided a Resident Expert with opportunities to observe other teachers, you may need to direct him or her to use these strategies. Keep in mind that many Resident Experts think they are already doing a good job, so they may not learn from observing a colleague unless you follow up with them. These directives should include clear expectations for the use of the new skills and strategies and a timeline for their integration. If you are working with a teacher who fits into the Challenged category, you will need to break the required skills into parts so the teacher can learn how to implement them. It might also be helpful to Challenged teachers to get follow-up assistance from peer coaches, instructional coaches, additional observations, and so on. If you have implemented sound support for the expectations and the teacher is still not able to implement them, you may need to consider whether the deficits are more than marginal.

If you are dealing with a veteran teacher and he or she is making very slow progress, you might consider the teacher deficient and move toward stronger discipline and possible termination. If you've spent a considerable amount of time and allocated resources to help the teacher improve, but she is still performing well below standards, she is a definite candidate for termination. If the teacher is a continuing contract teacher, you will need to document that you have provided him with clear information about his deficit areas and an opportunity to improve his performance before terminating his employment.

In many of the new teacher evaluation processes adopted by states, there is a provision for *intensive assistance*. In an intensive assistance program, a district uses an independent team to provide focused and specific assistance to teachers who are in danger of having their contracts terminated for ineffective teaching. Before nominating a teacher for the intensive assistance process, review the procedures for the process documented in the district's teacher evaluation policies. Also consider having a conversation with the human resources director, assistant superintendent, superintendent, or another administrator who deals with the details of the intensive assistance process in the district.

Political Influences in the Community

Schools and communities can be close knit. Some relationships have existed there long before you came and will still be there long after you leave. Teachers in your building may be friends with or relatives of others in the community. Information you tell one teacher may spread to others very quickly.

In our own experiences and the experiences of our colleagues, the connections and politics that operate in the community should be examined before moving forward. Supervisors who have been employed in the school or district for an extended period of time may already know about these relationships, but those who are relatively new to a school or district may need to conduct some research by talking informally with the superintendent, administrative assistants, cooks, custodians, or bus drivers and observing which parties socialize with each other. Gather this information about community relationships before there is an issue with a teacher, not when they are under scrutiny. Few people may want to talk with you once their friend, family member, or neighbor is placed on an improvement plan. In situations where an employee has connections to an influential person in the community, supervisors should consider moving slowly; providing ample assistance for the teacher; working with the superintendent, human resources director, or other district administrators to plan strategies to help the teacher improve; providing clear and definitive data documenting the areas of concern; and communicating to the teacher that you want to help him or her get better rather than just terminate the contract.

Time and Resources Available

Your availability to explain what needs to change and then following up to ensure the improvements are made are important factors when considering how to move forward with marginal teachers. If you work in a small school, by yourself, with especially limited time and resources, you may find it hard to make a significant impact in improving marginal teaching performance. If you have access to other peers, instruction or peer coaches, and professional development resources, the task is a little easier.

We have worked with many administrators who have attempted to address marginal teaching to terminate a contract without considering factors that could cause them problems. If you get in the middle of the process and an unanticipated problem comes up, it could negate all the hard work you have done to improve the situation or it could undermine your efforts and your credibility as a leader. Carefully thinking through and assessing the situation will save you valuable time and a potentially big headache.

It's important to plan ahead as much as possible so you can foresee and avoid problems before they occur, but in addition to planning, it's imperative that you possess a core set of skills in order to take on situations like this.

Skills for Addressing Marginal and Deficient Performance

In our experience working with marginal teachers and helping colleagues address teaching issues, we have observed that a core set of skills is required. In *Working With Difficult and Resistant Staff* (Eller & Eller, 2011), we describe these skills, which administrators need to effectively evaluate their employees. These skills are outlined in the following sections. Note that we have made significant revisions to this list to more accurately reflect marginal and deficient teacher evaluation.

Clear Understanding of the Teaching Performance Standards

As we have noted in earlier chapters, supervisors need to have a clear understanding of the teaching performance standards. It is important that supervisors articulate a clear and easy-to-understand definition of each of the teaching performance standards, examples of what they would see if a teacher were implementing these skills in a classroom, and examples of what it would look like if these skills were absent from a classroom. The definitions and examples should be divided into the major performance ratings outlined by the district. For example, if the teaching performance standards include the ratings of *does not meet*, *meets*, and *exceeds* standards, supervisors should be able to define and provide examples for each of those ratings. The tools and activities we provide in chapter 2 (page 21) will help you develop this understanding of expectations and skills.

Ability to Accurately Describe Deficit in Performance

This skill is dependent on an understanding of the teaching performance standards. In this skill, supervisors should be able to explain to marginal teachers the issue or problem in the performance and the impact this problem has on the classroom and the students. It's crucial that supervisors state the issue clearly. Vague or unclear descriptions may confuse the underperforming teacher. Before the teacher can improve his or her performance, he or she needs to understand the problem. It is important that the teacher also understands the recommended change and how the change will impact the students and the classroom.

At times, being able to clearly describe all of the teaching issues, their potential causes, and recommend strategies to improve the performance may be difficult to do using only classroom observational data. A supervisor may want to turn to alternative data sources that can verify the observational data.

Ability to Design an Appropriate Conference With the Employee

When addressing marginal and deficient teaching behaviors, it's important to plan and deliver a conference so you can identify the issues and put a plan in place for the improvement of the teacher's instruction. The most effective conferences have phases or steps in them to ensure that the teacher understands the areas of concern, the changes that need to be made, and the follow-up plan to ensure these changes take place.

For addressing marginal teaching, the exact phases or steps implemented are based on the type of teacher you are conferencing with. For example, with a Resident Expert, a supervisor may want to spend more time clearly addressing the needed changes and providing directives than trying to convince this teacher to accept his or her ideas. With a Challenged teacher, a supervisor may want to spend more time explaining the steps in implementing the new strategy than being directive. We'll talk in more depth later in this chapter about specific conferences based on marginal teacher types.

Refer to chapter 8 (page 119) for more information about conferencing, and see pages 197–205 in appendix B for templates to use when designing conferences to address different types of marginal or deficient teaching.

In our experiences working with marginal teachers or terminating contracts and in supporting supervisors who are facing these issues, we have found it is important that your conference plan is designed like a script. When putting together a script, you will need to include the exact words you will say when delivering the conference to the teacher. See chapter 8 (page 119) for more information on developing a script that can be used in an instructional conference.

Ability to Confront Employee About Performance

When supervisors have decided that the issues they see in the classroom are significant and consistent enough to be addressed, they need to bring them to the teacher's attention. It can be difficult to communicate a negative message to a teacher. Everyone likes to be nice and deal with positive aspects of supervision, but no matter how much a supervisor tries to soften the message, when the teacher hears that she is not performing well, she will most likely view the message as confrontational. This has been the case with most of the teachers we have had to share concerns with over the years. In rare cases, some express relief to know that they will be receiving help when we talk to them about their performance issues, but most take the message as negative and personal.

Supervisors need to prepare for defensive and emotional reactions and be ready for excuses, blaming others, emotional outbursts, and other negative reactions. If you expect these kinds of reactions, you won't be taken by surprise.

Ability to Address the Issue While Staying on Track

In many cases, when supervisors have to tell a teacher that he or she is not meeting the standards, the teacher will bring up other issues or try to provide excuses for the behavior. These off-track comments may take different forms based on the teacher type you are working with and the types of marginal behaviors you are addressing. For example, On-the-Job Retirees may try to remind you of their past service or how hard they worked in the past. Keep in mind that this is an effort to take you away from the original focus (the improvement of their behaviors) to a new focus (defending your rationale for addressing the performance issues). When working with deficient teachers, you'll want to consider strategies such as framing or setting up a tight agenda in order to stay on track.

Ability to Work Under Pressure

When supervisors address the marginal or deficient performance of one of their teachers, they should prepare to experience some pressure from the teacher and other members of the staff. It's a natural reaction for other teachers to support their colleagues when their teaching performance is being questioned. Some colleagues will feel sorry for the teacher even though they may have complained about his or her performance earlier. They may appeal to the supervisor to take it easy on the teacher in question or to try to understand things from the teacher's position as the supervisor helps remediate the teaching. If the supervision process moves toward termination, expect the pressure to be greater.

When addressing issues, supervisors should prepare for this pressure and seek ways to lessen the impact of the stress that will develop in these situations. Supervisors should get plenty of rest, decide what other tasks can be minimized or handled in other ways, use the skill of temporary suspension of opinion to keep the negative energy of others away, take stock in the positive aspects of the job, and think about how important it will be to address the performance concerns with the teacher.

Ability to Design and Implement Improvement and Follow-Up Plans

When working with marginal teachers, it is important to design improvement and follow-up plans that will provide the opportunity for them to learn the skills essential to improving their performance. The improvement plan should outline the activities, the expected level of performance, and the timeline required for the improvement of the marginal areas. The follow-up plan should include the strategies that will be used to ensure the integration of the new skills and strategies into the marginal teacher's instructional practice. Both the improvement plan and the follow-up plan may vary based on the skills the marginal teacher needs to change, the severity of the marginal skills, and the type of marginal teacher you are working with. Be sure to make these plans specific to the teacher's needs to increase the chances of success (Eller & Eller, 2010).

When working with performance concerns, keep in mind that even though the process may be moving toward contract termination, the supervisor will still need to continue helping the teacher improve his or her performance, which can be a tough balancing act. Supervisors need to be sure that any remediation plan they design and implement includes specific strategies and follow-up to ensure that the teacher has a chance to improve (Eller & Eller, 2010).

This kind of supervising takes a special skill set. Figure 9.1 provides a tool that supervisors can use to assess their abilities in each of the skills discussed in the preceding sections and develop plans to improve the skills that need strengthening.

The following template outlines some of the essential skills supervisors will need when working with teachers who have performance concerns. Use this template to assess your own level of skills within each area listed below. Read the specific skill outlined in each row. In column 2, rate your level of performance within each skill area. Finally, in column 3, list the strategies, professional development plans, or resources you will use to improve your skill in the areas that present a challenge for you.

Skill Required to Deal With Employee	Your Level of Skill in This Area (1–10; 1 = Very Limited, 5 = Somewhat Prepared, 10 = Very Prepared)	Strategy or Resource for Addressing Skill Limitation (Develop a plan for areas rated at a 6 or lower.)
Clear understanding of the teaching expectations		
Ability to accurately describe deficit in performance		
Ability to confront employee about performance		
Skill in addressing issue while staying on track		
Ability to work under pressure		
Ability to design and implement an improvement and a follow-up plan for the marginal teacher		

Source: Adapted from Eller & Eller, 2010.

Figure 9.1: Skill self-assessment template.

Conferencing Strategies to Address the Marginal Teacher Types

Let's examine how the conferencing template offered in chapter 8 (page 119) might be adjusted to work with marginal teachers. As we discuss the variations in the conferencing plans, we will also share our rationale behind these variations.

The Challenged

When developing conference plans to address teachers in the Challenged category, the emphasis should be on clearly explaining the expectations and then providing step-by-step guidance for making the needed changes. In *Working With Difficult and Resistant Staff* (Eller & Eller, 2011), we provide several templates to help administrators work with teachers fitting into the Challenged category. These templates involve breaking the required task into parts and then providing a clear explanation about how to implement the skills.

In general, Challenged teachers need the following from a supervisor during the conferencing process.

▸ Clear feedback on their teaching skills in relation to the defined standards of performance

▸ Specific evidence gathered from teaching observations about their effective performance and areas needing improvement; these data should contain descriptions of how learners respond to the teaching strategies that are implemented

▸ Clear expectations of what needs to be changed, the timeline for completing these changes, and the resources they can use to accomplish these changes

▸ The follow-up method you will use in working with them

The conference plan we offer provides the Challenged teacher with the clarity he or she needs in order to understand what must be changed about his or her teaching and the timeline for when the changes should be made. The last stage of this conference—the stage when the supervisor implements strategies to ensure that the major recommendations are applied in the classroom—includes the support and accountability necessary to increase the teacher's chances of success. Consult the "Conferencing Template for the Challenged" form in appendix B (pages 197–200) for a detailed outline of the conferencing process to use when planning and delivering conferences for Challenged teachers.

On-the-Job Retirees

Tailor the conference for an On-the-Job Retiree so it meets the teacher's needs and also clearly communicates necessary changes in his or her teaching. The focus should be on understanding what caused the teacher to fall behind. Consider how you might approach the situation without causing the teacher to lose face. In cases where the teacher doesn't appear to care about his or her performance, you'll need to find a way to motivate the teacher to care.

In general, On-the-Job Retirees need the following from a supervisor during the conferencing process:

▸ Involvement and engagement in analyzing their teaching

▸ Clear feedback on their teaching skills in relation to the defined standards of performance

▸ Specific evidence gathered from teaching observations about their effective performance and areas needing improvement; these data should be in the form of the learners' reactions to their teaching strategies

▸ Clear expectations of what needs to be changed, the timeline for completing these changes, and the resources they can use to accomplish these changes

▸ Commitment to improving or changing their practices

▸ The follow-up method you will use in working with them and supporting them through the change

The conference plan we offer outlines how a supervisor could approach helping On-the-Job Retirees improve their performance. A crucial aspect of the conference is engaging the teacher in both understanding the need to change and compelling him or her to commit to the change. If the teacher agrees, your job will be easier than if the teacher is resistant to the change. If the teacher is resistant, your conference may need to be more directive and include clear performance expectations and deadlines for improvement. Consult the "Conferencing Template for On-the-Job Retirees" form in appendix B (pages 200–202) for a detailed outline of the conferencing process to use when planning and delivering conferences for On-the-Job Retirees.

Resident Experts

When developing a conference for Resident Experts, keep in mind that you may not be able to convince them that they need to improve their teaching. Make sure they understand your expectations. Don't concentrate on getting them to agree with you or buy in to your directives. Some Resident Experts will listen and make the needed changes, but in most cases they will not believe you or will resist your recommendations. You may find more success providing directives with clear deadlines for their implementation.

In general, Resident Experts need the following from a supervisor during the conferencing process:

▸ A clear and direct outline of what will happen during the conference

▸ Clear feedback on their teaching skills in relation to the defined standards of performance

▸ Clear expectations of what needs to be changed, the timeline for completing these changes, and the resources available to assist them

▸ The message that you are serious and other consequences will follow if the concerns are not addressed within the established timeline

▸ An understanding that you will be following up to assist them and to check that they are making the required changes

Administrators can consult the "Conferencing Template for Resident Experts" form in appendix B (pages 202–205) for a detailed outline for conducting conversations with Resident Experts.

Suggestions for Tracking Teacher Performance

When you work with teachers, it's important to be able to identify patterns of behavior. This is most commonly done through classroom observations, but it can be achieved using a variety of data sources. Keeping track of performance issues lets you see emerging patterns and address them before other issues arise. Identifying a problem early may help you avoid a more negative situation later.

When performing your duties as a supervisor, it is easy to forget about instances that have happened in the past. Many supervisors have developed good record-keeping systems to track teaching performance. Figure 9.2 shows an example of a template for keeping track of potential issues so they can be recalled as needed. This completed sample will give you an idea of how you might use this sheet to track performance. This tool assumes that the supervisor will have regular opportunities to gather data through classroom observations, observations of other duties, and other data sources. Visit **go.solution-tree.com/leadership** for a blank version of this template that you can use in your work.

Teacher: *Jim Smith*

Date: *9/3* Brief summary of the teaching performance: *Students had trouble following directions. Teacher had to raise his voice to get attention.*	Date: *9/12* Brief summary of the teaching performance: *Students still having trouble staying on task. Teacher had to stop class to remind students of procedures. (I talked to teacher about the situation.)*	Date: *9/25* Brief summary of the teaching performance: *Students were taking a test when I stopped in the classroom. All were on task.*
Date: *10/10* Brief summary of the teaching performance: *Students were working in groups but several were off task. As the teacher was redirecting, several students continued to talk. (I met with the teacher to share my concerns about the situation.)*	Date: *10/13* Brief summary of the teaching performance: *Teacher had to redirect student behavior several times during the lesson. Many students were not listening. (Met with teacher to share concerns about his performance. Told teacher I have some concerns. Set up follow-up visit to look for a change in the teaching performance.)*	Date: *10/30* Brief summary of the teaching performance: *Did follow-up visit. Classroom management is still a concern. (Supervisor and teacher developed follow-up plan for improvement.)*
Date: _____ Brief summary of the teaching performance:	Date: _____ Brief summary of the teaching performance:	Date: _____ Brief summary of the teaching performance:
Date: _____ Brief summary of the teaching performance:	Date: _____ Brief summary of the teaching performance:	Date: _____ Brief summary of the teaching performance:

Figure 9.2: Sample performance tracking sheet.

Visit **go.solution-tree.com** *for a reproducible version of this figure.*

This tool can be helpful not only for remembering what performance issues a teacher has had but also for helping the supervisor keep track of performance problems in the event that the teacher does not improve and the supervisor begins to consider terminating the teacher's contract. The resource is designed for use by the supervisor—not for providing documentation for the teacher. Chapter 10 (page 155) provides more information about the documentation necessary if you are faced with this unfortunate situation.

A Look Back

As Tom prepared to meet with Marty, he designed an instructional conference to clearly explain exactly what he wanted Marty to do. In this conference, it became clear to Tom that Marty had some of the characteristics of a Challenged teacher. Marty's skill set was somewhat limited. Tom presented his feedback and ideas about how Marty could learn skills that would help him improve his teaching. Tom told Marty that he would tell him exactly how he was progressing and would also ask for Marty's feedback in the process.

At first, Marty wanted to blame his students for the situation, but Tom used temporary suspension of opinion and reflecting whenever Marty started to get upset. After Marty vented for a minute, he focused on the strategies and ideas that Tom shared. Throughout the school year, there were tense conferences between Tom and Marty, but they started to make progress on improving Marty's teaching. They saw that the time and effort they dedicated to the improvement process started to pay off as they observed the students' improved learning.

Chapter Summary

In this chapter, we have explored issues and strategies related to addressing marginal—and, in some cases, deficient—teaching performance. These strategies are designed to help you better identify poor teaching performance, the type of marginal teacher you might be dealing with, and considerations that you will need to take into account when attempting to remedy these issues.

As you reflect on the information you learned in this chapter, respond to the following questions.

▶ Describe your understanding of marginal teaching. How can you use this description to help you identify marginal teachers?

▸ How would you describe deficient performance? What are the attributes that you would focus on when classifying a teacher as deficient?

▸ Why is the ability to identify specific marginal types important to you as a leader? How do you think you can put this information into practice at your school?

▸ What is the importance of thinking through some of the conditions that might impact your work with marginal and deficient teachers? Identify two to three conditions present in your school or district that could be problematic if not addressed before you take on a marginal or deficient teaching situation.

Once you have clearly thought through the process for identifying marginal or deficient teaching, you can then think about how you might explain your perceptions through the use of the conference. The kinds of conferences that have the greatest impact in helping teachers improve are those that are instructional in nature. Unfortunately, these are not always successful. In the next chapter, you'll learn about the necessary processes for terminating an employment contract when a teacher's poor performance does not improve despite your best efforts.

chapter 10

Documenting the Contract Termination Process

It was a stressful day at Jones Middle School. Marjorie, the principal, had a meeting scheduled with Thomas, his union representative, and the human resources director, to let Thomas know that she was recommending that the board not renew his contract for the upcoming school year. Throughout the last two school years, Marjorie had worked closely with Thomas to help him improve his teaching. She had him work with an instructional coach, observe other teachers in his department, and work with the building mentor, and she spent considerable time with him to try to improve his performance. None of these strategies worked.

During the meeting, Marjorie reviewed all of the information she provided to Thomas, the resources she dedicated to helping him improve, and exactly where his skills were not meeting the standards of the district. After this meeting, the union representative asked to talk with Thomas for a few minutes. When Thomas and the union representative returned to the office, Thomas offered to resign his position before Marjorie took a recommendation to the board. Marjorie and the human resources director agreed to accept Thomas's resignation.

Meetings like this are not easy but are sometimes necessary. When teaching deficiencies become so prevalent that—despite our efforts to help the teacher develop his or her skills—learning is severely inhibited, we have to end the teacher's employment to ensure that students receive the high-quality instruction they deserve. In Marjorie's case, she did a nice job of meticulously gathering the documentation she needed to make her case.

These are skills no one wants to learn, but they come in handy when dealing with markedly poor teaching performance.

In many cases, supervisors can implement strategies that will help their teachers learn and improve their instructional skills. In some instances, however, the teacher does not improve. In these instances, supervisors should document the performance issues for contract termination. While terminating a teacher's contract can be a difficult experience for the supervisor and the teacher, the students and the school will benefit in the end. The stakes are high for student learning. If a teacher cannot help students be successful, a supervisor has no choice but to let that teacher go. At times, a teacher's poor performance can become a negative force in a school, causing others to join in or become disillusioned with teaching. One bad apple can spoil a barrel, so a supervisor needs to be able to remove those teachers who contribute to a negative school climate or a lack of student achievement.

Chapter Focus

Terminating a teacher's contract can be a difficult and time-consuming process to complete. In this chapter, you will learn about identifying and documenting deficient teaching behavior as you proceed toward the teacher's employment termination. Specifically, you will learn the following.

- ▸ What constitutes proper written documentation regarding teacher performance problems and attempts to help the teacher improve in order to ensure legal compliance

- ▸ Possible sources of documentation, including conference summaries, and how to use them to formally address a teacher's deficiency

Proper Written Documentation

As you begin to transition into the possibility of contract termination, it's important to keep written documentation. This documentation has a variety of uses, as we will see in the next section. Keep in mind that the information we provide here is designed to give you a brief introduction and overview. Be sure to work with your district human resources division and possibly a labor attorney for more precise information about the documentation requirements in your region or state. A good resource we have used in the past is William C. Carey's (1988) *Documenting Teacher Dismissal*. This book does a nice job of describing some of the critical attributes required in the documentation process.

Purposes of Documentation

Documentation, in general, can serve a variety of purposes. Carey (1988) identifies the following purposes, which we have expounded on to highlight the important roles that documentation of deficient teachers can serve.

▸ **Provides a written, objective artifact of events:** When you work with teachers who are candidates for contract termination, you'll need to provide clear documentation, based on data, that their performance is markedly below expectations. Written documentation is essential as you begin to build a case against a teacher.

▸ **Helps to visualize patterns:** Sometimes it can be difficult to see patterns of problems in a teacher's performance. Having the information in written form, such as a record like the one we provide in figure 9.2 (page 151), can shed light on any patterns that may exist.

▸ **Prevents future denial:** As a supervisor, you may have many conversations during the course of the school year with teachers. If the content of these conversations is not documented, teachers could deny that you talked with them about a concern. Providing a summary of these conversations helps prevent this problem.

▸ **Provides clarity, keeps misunderstandings to a minimum:** When you have expressed concerns in writing, it is much easier for everyone to have a clear understanding of the issues.

▸ **Aids in memory:** Over time, it's easy to forget about issues. Having written notes or documentation helps you recall significant events even if they occurred several months ago.

▸ **Provides information for a possible hearing:** Typically, an ending point for termination processes is some sort of a hearing. This hearing may occur at the board level or in the legal system if the teacher appeals earlier decisions. In these instances, written documentation is a major source of the information presented at the hearing.

▸ **Supports future evaluators:** You may have a situation in which the previous supervisor told you about a problem but never left any written documentation about this problem. Because continuing contract terminations may take several years to complete, written documentation you leave behind may benefit the future supervisor who wishes to continue what you started.

Standards for Written Documentation

In Carey (1988), three guiding questions are provided that will help you focus on documenting information. Carey suggests these questions are helpful to third-party examiners of documentation, but we find them helpful for supervisors trying to improve the clarity or focus of their documentation. We supplement Carey's three questions with explanations and examples in the following list.

1. **Did the evaluator provide evidence that the proper procedures were followed?** When constructing documentation, be sure that you state any procedures or processes you used or that were present during discussions. For example, if the union representative was present, state that in the documentation. If you provide the teacher with an opportunity to respond to your statements in the conference, be sure to state that in the documentation.

2. **Does the documentation reveal allegations that are sufficient to warrant dismissal?** This question is key because it helps establish that there was clarity in your feedback to the teacher. The "Conferencing Template for Working With Student Achievement Concerns" (page 193 of appendix B) includes a section stating that you should tell the teacher he or she is not meeting the district standards and explain why he or she is not meeting the standards. This level of clarity is designed to establish the fact that you explained the seriousness of the situation.

3. **Does the documentation demonstrate or prove the existence of these conditions?** This question requires tangible evidence that what you are alleging has occurred. The tangible evidence could be precise behavior descriptions, dates, times, places where the incidents occurred, and so on. The information required for this question is addressed in "Conferencing Template for Working With Student Achievement Concerns" (pages 193–194 in appendix B).

Possible Sources of Documentation

In most cases, the documentation required for dealing with deficient teachers and possibly moving toward contract termination comes from our conversations and conferences. When supervisors see or hear about an issue, they initially meet with the teacher and share the issue in a conversation or conference. Since a lot of our communication starts off as verbal in nature, it's important to capture the key points of these conversations. A good vehicle for this is a conference summary.

Conference Summaries

An effective tool in working with teachers to follow up on conferences about teaching performance is a conference summary. A conference summary is an accurate and detailed description of a conference and the major points discussed in the conference. A good conference summary acts as a record of the conference and allows the supervisor to build a case for the improvements needed. Keep the following considerations in mind when developing conference summaries.

▸ **Make sure the conference summary is accurate:** The conference summary must accurately reflect the main points discussed in the verbal conference. For example, "This is a summary of a conference I had with [name] on [date] to talk about my concerns in [performance area]. In the conference, I thanked [name] for meeting with me, provided an overview of the conferencing process, and then proceeded to provide [name] with feedback from my [date] observation. During this conference, I addressed my major concerns related to [name's] teaching performance. One concern shared was the off-task behavior of the students during the lesson. As [name] was presenting content related to the lesson topic, several students were writing notes and talking to each other. [Name] didn't appear to notice them and kept talking. Their conversations got louder, and it became hard for other students in the class to hear the information [name] was presenting. This is an issue I have talked to [name] about in the past, and it continues to be a problem."

▸ **Avoid general or vague language:** Be clear and accurate in your main points and descriptions. For example, "In the conference, I shared that [name] started the lesson I observed by sharing a personal story about budgeting. The story started out appropriately, but [name] kept telling details about a personal family situation. The students started to disengage in the description as evidenced by the fact that many of them began talking to other students near them, drawing on their notebooks, looking away from the teacher, and putting their heads on their desks."

▸ **Relate any performance feedback or assessments back to the core performance expectations:** When providing feedback in a conference, be sure to tie the feedback to the teaching performance standards. The feedback should give the teacher information related to how their performance compares to the teaching performance standards. For example, "I told [name] that the story was too long and contained information that was too personal for the students. I told [name] that this behavior was not appropriate and was not meeting the district expectations and standards in [performance area]."

▶ **Reflect the teacher's replies or comments accurately:** Normally the teacher will share his perspective about the supervisor's feedback during a conference. Make note of what the teacher says so you can include it in the conference summary. Accurately including the teacher's comments from the conference adds objectivity and strength to the summary because it serves as a record of the conversation. For example, "After I presented my feedback, I asked [name] to share his perceptions of the situation. He said that he didn't realize the story was getting too detailed and inappropriate for the students."

▶ **Provide any directives or recommendations, and include a timeline for their implementation:** Be sure to include any recommendations or directives related to improving performance that you have provided for the teacher. It's important to include these so that later the teacher can't deny that you told her she needed to address the situation. Including your recommendations will also help you keep track of or remember the seriousness of the situation. For example, "I directed [name] to immediately stop sharing detailed personal information and only share general information when using personal stories to illustrate classroom content. I said I would stop by his classroom to see how he is doing on this aspect within the next two weeks."

Figure 10.1 provides several sample conference summaries. You'll see that we use a slightly different tone as we write each of these summaries, which are dated and appear as a sequence over time. As you work to complete your conference summaries, you'll want to develop the appropriate tone for your situation. As you review the sample conference summaries, be sure to focus on the clarity of the message in each of them. Also, keep in mind that the conference summaries portray the observations of a teacher over time. Finally, you'll notice that the audience these summaries are written for varies. We purposely wrote one summary directed to the teacher while the other summaries are written for a more general audience. In some cases, the feedback may seem less personal if the summary is written for an unspecified audience and the supervisor is simply describing the situation. In other cases, the summary is more personal and directed to the teacher. Supervisors will determine the specific audience for each conference summary.

Conference Summary: September 12

This is a summary of the conference I had with Paul Howard on September 12 concerning a classroom visit I made on that same day. During the conference, I provided an overview of the conference agenda and asked the teacher for his perceptions of the lesson. Paul shared that he thought the lesson went pretty well but there were a few students who seemed off task. I agreed with Paul's assessment and provided the following feedback.

> *As Paul got into the informational part of the lesson, I noticed three students were talking among themselves toward the back of the room. Their voice levels caused some distraction for the rest of the students, so Mr. Howard raised his voice and continued on with the lesson. The off-task students just increased their voice level, which made it harder for the rest of the students to focus. Finally, Mr. Howard appeared to get angry and just yelled at the students. This stopped the commotion for a few minutes, but they started talking again when he turned away.*

In our conference, I shared my concern for Mr. Howard's classroom management in this situation. I suggested that he consider some proactive ways to manage the classroom and potentially disruptive students before they get out of line. I suggested that Paul consider the following strategies: meeting with the students privately before class to outline his expectations, walking over by students when they appear to be getting off track, and moving away from lecturing to more engaging activities such as group work.

After I shared these strategies, Mr. Howard said he thought they could be successfully implemented to improve the focus on classroom management. I said that I would be stopping by his classroom periodically over the next couple of weeks to check on the situation.

Conference Summary: October 10

This is a summary of the conference I had with you on October 10 to discuss an observation I conducted on the same day. During the conference, I provided an overview of the agenda and asked you for your perceptions of the lesson. In the conference, I provided feedback on an issue I had addressed earlier.

- In our conference on September 12, I shared my concern with some aspects of your classroom management. Even though you said that you understood what needed to be changed and felt the strategies I suggested were things that you could do, there is still off-task student behavior occurring in your lessons. In this lesson, you had the students working in groups, but some students were not working on the task you assigned. This was evidenced

---

Figure 10.1: Sample conference summaries.

Continued →

by the fact that they were giggling and pointing instead of writing like the other students. This off-task behavior continued for about ten minutes until you apparently became frustrated and got angry with the students. You stood in front of the class, raised your voice, and directed them to get back on track. They did get back on track, but your behavior interrupted the other students' work. The intervention only lasted for a few moments, and then the students started giggling and pointing again.

- In the conference, I shared my continued concern with this behavior. I also told you that I'm seeing these issues on a consistent basis. At this point, you're not meeting district standards in the area of the classroom environment, specification 3, managing student behavior. I need you to focus on improving your classroom management skills so you can improve your performance in this area. When I asked for your thoughts regarding classroom management, you said that this is an area that has been troubling you and you would like some help and assistance. In order to help you in this area, you agreed to do the following.

  - You will review information from the book *Classroom Management That Works* (Marzano, 2003).

  - You will work with the building mentor to help you utilize information from this book in your classroom.

  - You will assess your performance based on my feedback. (In order to help provide you with the timely feedback you'll need, I'll do weekly observations in your classroom. These observations may not occur for entire lessons but over a varied time in order for me to see you in a variety of situations. I'll meet with you and give you feedback after these observations.)

  - You said that you thought these strategies would be helpful to you in improving your classroom management. You also said that you would welcome my regular observations and feedback to help you assess your progress in the area of classroom management. We agreed that this plan would start at the beginning of the week of October 15.

Conference Summary: October 30

This is a summary of the conference I held with Paul Howard on October 30, concerning his progress on his work to improve classroom management and also in relation to a follow-up observation I conducted in his classroom on the same day. In this conference, I outlined the agenda for the conference and shared my perspectives on his progress in classroom management.

In the lesson observed on this date, classroom management was still a concern. Mr. Howard was conducting a large-group lecture. There were three small groups of students who were not paying attention or focusing on instruction. Mr. Howard continued to lecture even though the students were off track. He did walk back and stand by some of the off-track students, which improved their behavior, but they went right back to being off track as soon as he walked away. As I've observed in the past, he became frustrated and raised his voice to the whole class, telling them to get back on track. This interrupted the learning of all the students—even those who were previously on task. I shared with him that even though he has made some progress in improving his classroom management skills, his performance is still not meeting the district standards for the classroom environment, specification 3, managing student behavior. I told Mr. Howard that we need to make the improvement plan more formal. We scheduled a follow-up meeting for October 31 to begin developing a written improvement plan. I also told Mr. Howard that since this improvement plan was related to his teaching performance, he could have a union representative attend the meeting with him. He said he would think about this and let me know later in the afternoon on October 30 if he was going to have a union rep attend the meeting. I reminded Mr. Howard that the purpose of this meeting was to develop a written plan to help him improve his performance in the area of concern. He said that he appreciated me being honest with him and providing him with feedback on his performance.

Formal Notice of Deficiency

Some states, school districts, and supervisors are required to provide a formal notice of deficiency to teachers when the administration has serious concerns about their performance and is contemplating contract termination. Figure 10.2 provides a sample notice of deficiency so you can see how these documents are worded. Keep in mind that this example is only provided to give you an idea about the clarity and precision required in a formal notice. Consider working with your district human resources office or a labor attorney when developing specific notices of deficiency if they are required in your state.

Notice of Deficiency

October 5, 2014   Hand Delivered

Dear Mr. Harrison,

This letter constitutes a formal Notice of Deficiency issued to you pursuant to Minn. Statutes 122A.40, subdivision 9 and specific directives that you are required to comply with. It has been prepared for the purpose of advising you, in writing, of certain actions and practices that are inappropriate and must be discontinued and areas in which your performance must improve.

You are hereby directed to correct the deficiencies cited herein, to refrain from the inappropriate practices listed, and to comply with all of the directives contained in this letter. Failure to do so may result in further disciplinary action, which may include termination of your employment with the school district.

The specific areas of deficiency are: neglect of duty, or persistent violation of school laws, rules, regulations, or directives; any deficiency; conduct unbecoming a teacher which materially impairs the teacher's instructional effectiveness; and other good and sufficient grounds rendering you unfit to perform your duties consisting of, but not limited to, the following.

Figure 10.2: Example of a formal notice of deficiency.   Continued →

1. Failure to develop and support relationships with regular education teachers serving your students.

   - On September 9, the principal, Ms. Charles, talked with you about the need to meet with regular education teachers serving your students to set up collaborative planning sessions. In this meeting, you said you understood the importance of this directive and would meet with these teachers to set up these meetings.

   - On September 25, the principal, Ms. Charles, met with you again to check on the progress of these meetings. In this meeting, you said that you had not had a chance to set up these collaborative meetings but would do so as soon as possible. Ms. Charles directed you to schedule these collaborative meetings by the end of September. This directive has not been completed.

2. Failure to properly assess the progress of your students within their academic and social skill areas.

   - On September 15, Ms. Charles talked with you about the lack of accurate assessment information available on your students. Ms. Charles noted the difficulties that had occurred in two recent staffings as a result of this lack of information. On this date, Ms. Charles directed you to submit current assessment information related to individualized education program (IEP) goals and objectives of your students by the end of September. As of this date, those assessment reports have not been submitted as directed.

You are hereby directed as follows:

You must immediately schedule collaborative planning meetings with those teachers who serve your students. At these meetings, you must develop comprehensive plans to work with these teachers to enhance the performance of the students you're responsible for serving. These plans need to be a direct match with their IEP goals. In addition to these plans, you must develop a schedule from now until the end of the current school year for regular assessment and planning meetings with these teachers to discuss your students' progress and future goals. You must also document the specific plans made during these meetings. All of these directives need to be completed in writing and submitted in a timely manner to the building principal, Ms. Charles. The scheduling of meetings needs to be submitted by October 30, and the summaries of the planning meetings need to be submitted within one week of each planning meeting.

You must develop a plan to assess all the students under your care in addition to their IEP goals. This plan must be submitted to your building principal, Ms. Charles, by October 30. In addition to your plan, you must submit a copy of these assessment results showing how they match your students' IEP goals within one week of completing these assessments.

Within both of these directives, you need to complete them by the outlined dates. If you determine that you're unable to do this without assistance, you need to submit a written plan to your building principal describing your difficulty and your need for specific assistance.

If you have any questions regarding these activities, please address them to your building principal.

Failure to follow these directives will result in further disciplinary action up to and including discharge from your employment with the school district.

Sincerely,

[Note: This sample letter of deficiency is provided only as an illustration. Consider seeking legal assistance for developing specific letters of deficiency in your school or district.]

A formal notice of deficiency allows a supervisor (and, in essence, the school district) to formally inform the teacher that there are serious performance concerns. Notices of deficiency are normally based on several observations and conferences in which the supervisor has clearly described the issues related to the identified performance concerns. In some settings, formal notices of deficiency also set intensive assistance processes in motion. They need to be written so the teacher clearly understands the concerns and the expectations for the improvement of their instruction.

A Look Back

At the beginning of this chapter, we learned that Marjorie compiled extensive documentation to show Thomas's deficits, her efforts to remediate his performance issues, and that he was still clearly performing significantly below district standards. If she had not done such a thorough job in her documentation, Thomas likely would not have resigned and would have fought her recommendation to terminate his contract. In this case, consistently using multiple forms of documentation helped increase the likelihood of a smooth termination process.

Clearly documenting teacher performance does not guarantee an easy resolution when dealing with deficient performance issues, but it will help to accurately document the progression of a supervisor providing the teacher with information about his or her performance, strategies to improve, and consequences if the needed improvement does not occur. These factors ensure a fair and objective process that benefits the teacher, the supervisor, and the students. This is what supervisors need to model in all of their dealings with others.

Chapter Summary

In this chapter, we have explored the necessary processes for pursuing contract termination of deficient teachers to help you be more prepared as you approach serious performance situations. If you have not thought through the process for documenting your concerns about and interactions with deficient teachers, you may be surprised by the complexity of the situation once a decision has been made to terminate the teacher's employment.

As you reflect on the information you learned in this chapter, respond to the following questions.

▸ Why is documenting deficient performance essential for termination proceedings?

▸ How can you gather the written documentation you need to move the termination process forward?

While termination discussions and proceedings are not a highlight of an administrator's job, ensuring that you have the necessary documentation throughout the process will make it more efficient and will help avoid a drawn-out process—which will benefit everyone involved. Thorough documentation of deficient teaching can help you feel confident in your decision to terminate a contract and ensure that students receive the quality instruction they need to be successful. In the next chapter, you'll explore the major components and processes of the final summative evaluation of teachers at the end of the evaluation cycle.

chapter 11

Conducting and Delivering Summative Evaluations

In chapter 1 (page 5), we discussed the two major aspects of the teacher appraisal process—supervision and evaluation. As the year progresses and supervisors analyze the various data sources that contribute to each teacher's performance, they should provide periodic feedback and support to the teachers. This type of evaluation is called *formative*. In a classroom setting, teachers use formative assessments to help students see where they are in relation to performance expectations and to keep them moving forward (if they are on track) or make changes (if they are not meeting expectations). Formative evaluations of teacher performance do the same for teachers: supervisors are periodically (and regularly) giving teachers information about their performance.

The other type of evaluation is *summative*. In a classroom setting, teachers use information they have gathered during the term to assign a final or summative grade. These grades may be based on multiple data sources or performance demonstrations that have varying levels of emphasis and importance. The same process holds true for teachers and their summative evaluations. In a summative evaluation, supervisors analyze the various data sources related to a teacher's performance and develop a final score or grade. The supervisors then combine the data to form a complete picture of the teacher's performance. Since a summative evaluation comes at the end of a period of time (typically at the end of a school year), there is a finality to the evaluation. The supervisor provides a "grade" for the teacher's performance based on multiple data sources and multiple performance demonstrations that have varying levels of emphasis and importance. The supervisor, in much the same fashion as a teacher, develops the summative evaluation by carefully weighing the levels of performance and the importance of the tasks. We provide several vignettes throughout this chapter to illustrate varying aspects that are all important to consider when conducting summative evaluations. Note the way the supervisor in the following scenario, for example, weighs multiple pieces of information in her summative evaluation.

> *Jan, a middle school principal, was getting ready to do the planning for her end-of-year summative conferences with the teachers who were on formal review cycle this year. She was working to put together all of the data and make judgments about the overall performance of her teachers.*
>
> *One of her teachers, Eric, had made some good gains in his teaching skills, but his student achievement scores were a little lower than Jan would have liked. He had been working with a particularly difficult class that had academic trouble in the past. In watching several lessons and analyzing some of his other performance areas, Jan determined that Eric was on the right track with his job performance.*
>
> *As she reviewed his teaching performance, she could see that Eric had made some good gains in several areas on the performance evaluation, especially in his ability to develop positive relationships with his students. This was an area that would help him improve student performance in the future. Because of the strength of the other areas in Eric's evaluation, Jan decided to help Eric set a professional goal in the area of improving student achievement but not let this area impact his overall summative evaluation.*

In this example, we can see that Jan understands the complexities of Eric's situation. If she had overreacted to one data source when determining Eric's effectiveness, she may have missed an opportunity to contribute to his growth. As we supervise teachers and evaluate their performance, we need to look at the entire scope of what they do.

Chapter Focus

In this chapter, we will focus on the summative evaluation process for teachers. The summative or end-of-year process is different from the day-to-day feedback processes used in teacher evaluation. The processes you use to analyze and communicate the levels of performance need to be tailored to the summative process. As a result of reading this chapter, you'll learn the following.

▶ Contributing factors for summative evaluations, such as quality of performance and alignment of performance areas with student needs

- How to incorporate multiple data sources when documenting summative performance
- Levels of performance and experience to help you record teachers' growth in various areas
- Caveats for scoring varied performance expectations and experience
- The importance of teacher involvement in gathering evidence and reflecting on progress
- Key elements of summative evaluation conferences, such as allowing time to explain the data and rationale behind the score a teacher has earned during the course of the year

Contributing Factors for Summative Evaluations

There are several factors supervisors must consider when developing summative evaluations. We discuss these in the following sections.

Quality of Performance

As you analyze the performance of the teacher throughout the school year, you'll need to assess the level of performance in comparison to the expectations. If the expectation for teachers is that they will consistently involve all students in processing information during a lesson, and the teacher is not meeting this expectation, then the summative score will reflect this level of performance. If a teacher involves students by having them conduct the lesson while the teacher facilitates the lesson, they may be operating above expectations. If a teacher lectures without any processing by the students, that teacher may be rated below the district standard.

Quality Versus Quantity

Evaluators need to consider when analyzing performance and developing summative scores the quality of the performance versus the quantity of performance and the number of times a particular performance level has been demonstrated. For example, if a high performance level has only been demonstrated occasionally, should it receive the same merit in a summative evaluation as it would if it were demonstrated regularly? We say no. In a summative evaluation, a performance level must be demonstrated a sufficient number of times. That number is relative and based on a supervisor's judgment. One outstanding performance should not outweigh twenty subpar performances. If a skill is poorly demonstrated consistently and effectively implemented only occasionally, how should it be weighed in relation to the summative evaluation? In our opinion, the summative score should reflect a lower rating because the lower performance level was more prevalent than the higher performance level. Thus, the summative score should be a reflection of the most prevalent performance level, so that is a more accurate representation of the teacher's normal performance.

Relationships Between Performance Factors

The connection or relationship between performance areas is also an important consideration when completing the summative evaluation. If a teacher does a good job building positive relationships with the students and also exhibits effective classroom management, how should the teacher's summative score be determined? When related skills are effective, they tend to become more powerful and have a greater impact than if those skills were implemented alone. The relationship between the areas should factor into the scoring or summative evaluation of a teacher.

Alignment of Performance Areas and Needs of the Students

In classrooms and schools, the needs of the students can vary. When teachers implement skills or strategies that better meet these needs, it may make their summative scores rise. For example, if students show they are lacking organizational strategies, and their teacher analyzes data to identify this need and works to correct it, the supervisor may weigh these essential skills more heavily in helping to determine the final summative score than if the teacher were displaying another, less important strategy. In other words, those skills and strategies deemed essential in a school based on the needs of the students may hold more weight in the final score than skills and strategies not deemed as important.

Use the template in figure 11.1 as you consider these factors and analyze and assess your teachers' performance.

Multiple Data Sources

When considering a rating within a performance area, it's also important to look at multiple data sources. For example, if you want to assess how well the teacher helps students learn, you'll want to examine student achievement data, student perceptions of the classroom, how the teacher presents information to the students, how the teacher manages the learning environment, and other related factors.

Consider the following factors when determining summative ratings for your teachers. Think about each factor as you analyze the data and information related to teacher performance.

Quality of Performance How does this teacher's performance in an area compare to the expectations for the entire faculty? (At the highest performance level, the teacher is exhibiting skills that few other teachers are exhibiting.)	1 = Behind others, 10 = Model for others 1 2 3 4 5 6 7 8 9 10
Quantity of Performance How frequently is the high-level performance exhibited? (At the highest performance level, the skill is demonstrated constantly in a variety of settings.)	1 = Occasionally, 10 = Constantly 1 2 3 4 5 6 7 8 9 10
Relationships Between Performance Factors What is the connection or relationship between the high-level performance areas? (At the highest performance levels, the skills are directly related or connected to each other.)	1 = Unrelated, 10 = Related or Connected 1 2 3 4 5 6 7 8 9 10
Alignment of Performance Areas and Needs of the Students How well do the high-level performance areas match the student learning needs? (At the highest performance levels, the skills are an exact match to the needs of the students.)	1 = Isolated or Unrelated, 10 = Directly Related to Needs 1 2 3 4 5 6 7 8 9 10

How well does the teacher do in relation to the attributes listed here?

How does his or her overall performance within an area compare to others in the building? Could this teacher serve as a model for others?

Figure 11.1: Factors to consider when determining a summative rating.

*Visit **go.solution-tree.com/leadership** for a reproducible version of this figure.*

In chapter 1, we introduced the concept of alternative data sources. See figure 1.2 (page 15) to review the alternative data sources we discussed earlier. The information in figure 1.2 can be helpful as we consider the total performance of the teacher. The stronger (either positive or negative) summative ratings should be based on the analysis of multiple data sources. Multiple data help justify these stronger ratings because the data show a broader scope of work related to the teaching standards. For example, if a teacher is doing an outstanding job working positively with parents, the supervisor can document this using parent notes, informal conversations with parents, the number of parent volunteer hours in that teacher's classroom, the number of parent requests for students to be assigned to that teacher, and so on. Each of these data sources may seem minor, but the combination reflects good performance for this teaching standard. Let's see how this applies in the following example.

> Todd, a high school principal, is working with Charles, a mathematics teacher, in the formal evaluation cycle. As he reviews some of the information related to Charles's performance in the area of improving student learning, he notes that Charles's classes have the highest scores on the state mathematics test. When further examining other data sources, Todd remembers that in his observations, he had some concerns about the authoritarian way Charles managed his classroom. He also noticed that Charles sent out the highest number of academic warning letters to students who were in danger of not passing his class each midquarter and had a high number of office referrals.

> Even though he had high standardized test results, other factors indicated that the learning environment in Charles's classroom was not healthy for students. In analyzing the various data sources, Todd found that Charles's performance in this area was not meeting the district standards.

This type of situation can be common in schools. Teachers might be able to produce student achievement results but at the expense of other crucial aspects of student learning. In this example, Charles may be able to make good achievement gains but could be harming students as a result. Todd needs to weigh all of the factors and then determine the total rating of the teacher.

But what if you are trying to document an outstanding or superior level of performance by a teacher? Multiple data sources can work together to provide more weight or power to the performance area. Let's see how this works in the following example.

Sue built a strong learning environment in her classroom over many years. Her students were always on task and conscientious. She had a seamless way of moving from topic to topic. She was always able to develop strong working relationships with her parents and engage them in her classroom. Overall, she was seen as child centered and a positive staff member.

As Thomas, her principal, approached her evaluation, he wanted to find a way to both document and describe what made Sue such a good teacher. He met with Sue and talked about what he saw as he observed her classroom instruction, and he noted that he never had the opportunity to see other areas where Sue worked to build this sense of community. He asked Sue to gather some of the feedback she had received from parents about their children's experiences in her classroom. He also asked Sue to share lesson plans that reflected how she had developed student independence in her classroom. Finally, Thomas reviewed the feedback the students provided through a classroom climate survey. All of the data sources confirmed Thomas's observations regarding classroom climate.

When the time came to complete her summative evaluation, Thomas was able to combine the data sources to show that Sue:

- *Implemented strategies and produced results that exceeded the district's expectations and could be used as a model for others*

- *Consistently and regularly implemented these model strategies*

- *Exhibited model strategies documented using a variety of data sources*

He used this combination of sources to document why he rated Sue as exemplary in the areas of meeting student needs, effectively managing classroom procedures, and building an effective classroom community.

As you can see, connecting multiple data sources can help you identify and document exemplary teacher skills or performance. Multiple data sources also help the teacher see and understand all aspects that contribute to the performance area. As a supervisor, use positive examples like this as a road map to help other teachers reach a similar level of performance. Keeping track of the various data sources can also help you generate examples when faculty members ask, "What are you looking for in the area of _____?"

The template in figure 11.2 will help you identify and analyze data sources to document performance levels.

When attempting to document or justify performance ratings for teachers, it can be difficult to keep track of the various data sources that relate to a performance area. Use the following template to help you track these data sources.

Teacher: _____   Grade or subject: _____

Performance area or areas: _____

Performance Area	Data Source	Data Source	Data Source	Data Source

Figure 11.2: Connecting or combining data sources to document performance ratings.

Visit **go.solution-tree.com/leadership** *for a reproducible version of this figure.*

Levels of Performance and Experience

As you examine your teaching performance standards, you may notice that the rubric of teacher performance expectations is focused on different levels of performance. These different levels may be expressed the same way for all teachers. For example, in the area of classroom management, the performance level for those meeting the standard might be listed as "the teacher effectively organizes the classroom for effective instruction." However, we may have a higher level of expectation for an experienced teacher than a new or novice teacher who may still be developing skills in this area but is performing at an expected level for his or her experience.

It's important to keep the level of experience in mind as we think about rating or evaluating each teacher's performance. In general, teachers can be expected to improve as they gain more experience. It's true that, at times, schools hire teachers who can immediately exhibit effective strategies and skills, but most teachers experience a learning curve as they spend more time teaching, acclimate to the school, get to know the needs of their students, and so on.

As supervisors work with these teachers in both the supervision (growth aspects) and evaluation (measuring aspects) of their job performance, they should take level of experience into account. By considering the level of performance and how it relates to the experience level of the teacher, supervisors are in a better position to be fair when assessing a teacher's performance. Note how this plays out in the following example.

> Myrna, the principal of Washington Middle School, was working with Miriam, a new teacher. At the beginning of the year, Myrna held an orientation meeting where she distributed the district's teacher evaluation informational booklet. This informational booklet outlined the timelines and processes for the teacher evaluation process. It also contained a rubric that provided descriptions for the various teaching performance standards. Miriam has reviewed the informational handbook and is ready for her classroom observations with Myrna.

> Miriam was still learning the processes when Myrna came to conduct her first performance observation. In the conference that followed, Myrna shared her perceptions of the lesson. She shared positive feedback but pointed out Miriam's need for improvement in the area of classroom management. Myrna encouraged Miriam to work with the instructional coach to improve her classroom management.

> As the year progressed, Myrna provided Miriam with positive feedback about her changes in classroom management. Miriam was making gains in this area but was nervous that she was not consistently reaching the meets district standards level on the teaching rubric.

> During the summative conference, Myrna shared with Miriam that she was pleased with her growth in her classroom management skills. Myrna said that even though Miriam was still learning and growing in the area of classroom management, she was performing at an appropriate level for a new teacher. Myrna also noted that she expected Miriam to make even more growth in this area during the next school year.

In this example, we see how Myrna adjusted her expectations for Miriam in her first year of teaching based on Miriam's experience level. Even though she adjusted expectations for the first year, she was clear in the summative conference that she expected Miriam to continue to grow during her second year at the school. When making adjustments based on experience levels, it's important to communicate your expectations for continued growth in the future.

In order to factor experience into the evaluation and supervision processes, think about performance expectations and plot them out based on different levels of experience as you work with teachers. Table 11.1 illustrates possible performance expectations in the area of classroom management based on level of experience.

Table 11.1: Example of Performance Expectations and Years of Experience for Meeting District Standards in Classroom Management Criteria

Component	1–2 Years of Experience	3–5 Years of Experience	5 or More Years of Experience
Classroom Management—Meeting District Standards	• Has a basic understanding of effective classroom management principles • Uses this understanding to react to classroom disruption • Has periodic or regular classroom disruptions	• Understands classroom management strategies • Uses classroom management strategies to prevent classroom disruptions • Organizes classroom to minimize issues • Actively teaches classroom procedures • Builds a community of learners	• Understands and utilizes effective strategies to proactively deal with classroom management • Actively teaches classroom processes and procedures • Involves the students in managing some aspects of the classroom • Dedicates minimal time to management issues

*Visit **go.solution-tree.com/leadership** for a reproducible version of this figure.*

Keep in mind that this example is for illustrative purposes only. In some settings, the expectations will be much different. For example, in a setting where there are many opportunities for students to get distracted or off task, it may be crucial for a new teacher to operate at a very high level in the area of classroom management. In other settings, there may be more time for the teacher to gain the necessary skills. Visit **go.solution-tree.com/leadership** to access the blank reproducible "Template for Identifying Performance Expectation Levels

Based on Experience" to use in determining your performance expectations based on the experience levels of your teachers.

Caveats for Scoring Varied Performance Expectations and Experience

As logical as it may seem to vary expectations based on the experience levels of teachers, there are some limitations with this strategy. Keep the following in mind if you choose to implement varied performance expectations based on levels of experience.

- In your leadership encounters, you have likely developed a track record for what you expect to see teachers accomplishing at various levels of experience. Yet, it's important to keep your established varied performance expectations from overriding your instincts and knowledge if you believe a teacher is capable of more than his or her years in the profession may indicate. If you use the teaching performance standards in the selection process, you may see advanced skill levels in your newer employees. If you think they have well-developed skills, work with them to bring out their best. Don't communicate that it's OK for them to perform at the beginning levels if they are capable of performing at higher levels. If they do perform at levels higher than expected for their experience, they might deserve an above average or exceptional summative rating.

- Be careful about communicating these expectations to your teachers as a group. In the past, colleagues told us they were going to develop desired levels of performance and then duplicated this list and distributed it to their teachers. Identifying experience-appropriate performance levels is a tool for you to use in your supervision, but you may actually lower the performance of some teachers if you say, "All teachers with less than five years of experience should be at [name the level]." Some of them may decide that it's OK if they only reach the minimum levels of performance.

- Make varied levels a minimum—not a maximum—expectation. As you work with your teachers, the varied performance levels should be a starting point for your supervision and coaching. As a supervisor, your job is to help teachers move toward the highest levels of performance based on the teaching performance standards.

Identifying the desired expectations based on levels of experience is a good way to provide your teachers with reasonable guidelines for their performance, but it's important that you are careful not to lower expectations for exceptional teachers in the process.

Teacher Involvement in Gathering Evidence and Reflecting on Progress

Evaluators and supervisors cannot possibly know everything about the total performance of their teachers. Robert Marzano and Michael Toth (2013) discuss these unobserved data and how they can contribute to measurement error in the evaluation process, noting that even a conscientious supervisor who spends a lot time visiting classrooms can only see small parts of the total amount of teaching that occurs during the course of a school year. Thus, in working with a majority of your teachers, it's helpful to involve them in their own evaluation. By engaging in the evaluation process, your teachers will understand the various elements and the criteria used in it.

There are many ways to involve teachers in gathering data to document their teaching performance. Some evaluators hold a planning conference at the beginning of the process to set goals and begin the data-gathering process. Others meet with their teachers during the year to set up data-gathering opportunities once they notice patterns in performance emerge.

Whatever method you use, it's a good idea to involve teachers in gathering data to document their performance ratings. In figure 11.3, we provide a letter that one principal uses to inform her teachers of the opportunity to be a partner in the evaluation process by providing data in areas she does not include in her observations. Gathering data samples could be similar to the portfolio process described chapter 5 (page 83), or it could be less formal, with the teacher providing incidents and examples to help justify the summative score.

Summative Evaluation Conferences

Holding a summative evaluation conference is critical for both you and the teacher. In the summative evaluation conference, you get an opportunity to explain the data and rationale behind the score or evaluation the teacher has earned during the course of the year. Key aspects of the conference are described in the following sections. Clarifying teachers' strengths and the growth needed in the future will help them learn more about their teaching.

Name: _____ Date: _____

As your principal, I know many of you are implementing strategies, conducting innovative instructional practices to meet the needs of students, and engaging in professional growth areas. Many of your examples are things I cannot easily see in my classroom observations, my analysis of your professional growth goals, or the other data sources available to me.

I'd like to get your perspective on other areas that you feel contribute to your success as a teacher. Please complete the following form, and return it to me by _____. Once I receive your form, I'll schedule a meeting to talk with you about your examples and how they might be used in the summative evaluation process.

1. List any schoolwide committees you have served on, and explain your role.

2. List any school activities you have initiated or participated in that have enhanced the school's image.

3. List any workshops or in-services you have attended.

4. List any opportunities you have provided for students to receive extra academic assistance.

5. List any professional conferences you have attended.

6. List any university course work or degree programs you have completed this school year.

7. List any leadership roles (within or outside the building) you have assumed this year.

8. List any grant proposals you have submitted.

9. List any professional articles submitted for publication.

10. Indicate any professional organizations you belong to or serve on in a leadership capacity.

11. Include any other pertinent information related to your performance that might be important for me to know.

Sincerely,
[Name]

Figure 11.3: Sample letter asking teachers for performance evaluation data.

Explaining the Data Used to Justify the Rating

It can be difficult to explain the reasoning, rationale, or justification for the summative rating. The best way to do this is to outline the various data sources used to determine this rating. Make sure your justifying statements contain the following three key messages.

1. The rating or level of performance the teacher earned

2. The data sources used to document the rating

3. How the data sources illustrate the level of performance

The following statements demonstrate these three key messages being communicated.

1. "You earned a rating of exemplary in the area of organizing the learning environment. In documenting your performance in this area, I used the data from my classroom observations, the informal observations I have made of your students, data from the student perception surveys administered in your classroom, the data you provided about how you developed this high level of management, and the data you provided about parental feedback obtained in the parent-teacher conferences. All of these data sources indicated that your performance is exemplary and something that I could use as a model for others in the building."

2. "As I reflect back to your performance for the year, in the area of improving student learning, you earned a rating of meets district standards. In documenting your performance in this area, I used information from the latest state testing, which your students performed well on; my observations of your instruction, in which I noted that you were very clear and thorough in explaining concepts to the students; and your professional growth goal, in which you established a focus to work with your instructional coach to improve the clarity of your presentations. All of these data sources indicated that you are meeting the high standards of the district in this area."

3. "In relation to your summative rating for this school year, I rated you as growing and learning in the area of assessing student learning. In examining the various data sources associated with this area, I saw that you have worked hard with the mathematics coach to design and implement assessments. I noted in my observations that you do a nice job presenting information that students will need in order to improve their achievement in mathematics. I saw from the curriculum units you provided that you are improving the follow-up strategies you use with students based on the assessments. I see that you have made good progress, and I need you to continue this progress next year so we can look at documenting your performance as meeting district standards."

These three examples are provided to give you a picture of how the rationale for a performance rating might sound in an actual conference. Keep in mind that you will want to make sure the justification you share in your conferences fits into your natural communication style. Also, it needs to be communicated in a way that will be understood and accepted by the teacher.

Framing Summative Rating Comments

In delivering summative ratings, it's a good idea to think about how you state the feedback for the teacher. For example, if you say, "You are performing at the high level the district expects," you frame the feedback as a positive message. If you say, "I only rated you as *meets district standards* in the area of _____," you imply that the performance is substandard. Stating, "I know you have worked hard in the area of engaging students and you are meeting the high standards of the district," however, sends a positive message that the teacher's work is reflective of the district's standards. How you deliver the rating message can sometimes be more important than the actual performance rating. Keep this in mind as you prepare to deliver summative performance messages to your teachers.

For more help structuring evaluation conferences, see pages 205–207 in appendix B for the template titled, "Conferencing Template for Summative Evaluations," which includes sample statements. You can also visit **go.solution -tree.com/leadership** for a blank version of the template to help you plan a summative evaluation conference by clearly explaining the scores, strengths, and potential growth areas to your teachers.

Chapter Summary

In this chapter, we discussed summative evaluation. A summative evaluation is the final assessment or score the teacher earns as a result of the evaluation process. It is different from the day-to-day evaluation of the teacher because it is a summation of the data and the efforts in the teacher evaluation process.

As you reflect on the information you learned in this chapter, respond to the following questions.

▸ What is the difference between formative and summative evaluations? How does knowing these differences help you better work with your teachers?

▸ Why do we want to examine the concepts of quality versus quantity when developing ratings in the summative evaluation process? How does understanding these concepts help evaluators develop more accurate and valid summative ratings?

▸ How does framing the summative rating help keep the summative conferencing process focused and positive? What are some common terms or language you can use that will help the teacher see the positive in ratings that may appear to be average or normal?

As you work with your teachers to effectively implement the evaluation process, we hope you'll find the strategies and techniques presented in this book helpful. We know each person and situation is different and must be approached in a unique manner, but many evaluators have used the ideas and techniques presented here with great success over the years.

Evaluating and supporting teachers is one of the most important tasks supervisors do each year. We wish you well as you implement this key aspect of instructional leadership.

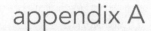

Forms and Templates to Guide the Coordination of PLC and Teacher Evaluation Process

Consider using the following forms and templates as you connect PLC work to the teacher evaluation process. Each of the forms and templates contains a brief explanation of how the resource could be used.

School Improvement Goals and Actions

The following form for school improvement or PLC goals and expected actions (figure A.1) provides teachers with clear expectations for the PLC process. This form can be used in a goal-setting or planning meeting at the beginning of the cycle. Note that the figure refers to an additional tool—the Fall PLC Goal-Setting Plan—to use simultaneously. See figure A.2 (page 185) for this item.

The professional learning community will work collaboratively to do the following.

Action (Goal-Setting Process)	How (Use Fall PLC Goal-Setting Document)
Analyze multiple data points for incoming students to help answer the question, Who are our students?	Access data from tests and assessments for incoming students. (Question 1 on the Fall PLC Goal-Setting Plan)
Create instructional model/classes/groups based on these data points, and determine who is teaching each class or group.	Based on the data, group students according to instructional level, and identify who is teaching each level. (Question 2 on the Fall PLC Goal-Setting Plan)

Figure A.1: School improvement goals, PLC goals, and expected actions of PLCs form.

Continued →

Write a SMART goal based on the building or district goals.	Using results from last year and current student data, write a SMART goal based on the building or district goals. (Questions 3–4 on the Fall PLC Goal-Setting Plan)
Determine the visible learning strategies (as defined by John Hattie [2012] in his book *Visible Learning for Teachers*) that will be used to meet the needs of the students.	Identify the visible learning strategies that will be most effective with students, and determine what professional learning is needed for teachers to deliver these strategies. (Question 5 on the Fall PLC Goal-Setting Plan)
Decide what measures the PLC will use to determine how students are performing.	Focus on using tools that measure increased student achievement and data from assessments to improve instruction (practice and performance) measures. (Question 6 on the Fall PLC Goal-Setting Plan)
Define a communication/feedback plan that answers the questions: a. How will students know where they are and how to move forward? b. How will families know where students are and how to move forward? c. How often and by what means will this information be communicated?	Engage in early goal setting meetings with students and families. Use the PLC to help with the goal setting for students. Include meaningful, consistent feedback to students and families. Each year, engage in review of students' progress with the student and family. (Questions 7–8 on the Fall PLC Goal-Setting Plan)
Engage in collegial peer observation to provide feedback to teachers about the delivery of the visible teaching strategies.	Three times a year: • Determine what processes will be used (video, read time) for observations. • Determine how feedback will be provided using collegial instructional coaching processes. (Question 9 on the Fall PLC Goal-Setting Plan)
Maintain a digital portfolio documenting the work of the PLC.	Determine how the PLC and individuals within the PLC will document the work of the PLC.

Source: Form created by Angie Peschel. Used with permission.

Use the goal-setting planning document in figure A.2 to help teachers plan how they might coordinate their PLC work with their teacher evaluation activities and goals.

Grade level / content area: _____

Job-alike collaborative team members: _____

State-, building-, or district-level goals: _____

Goal Setting

1. What do the data points tell you about your students this year?

2. What are the instructional groups that need to be created based on these student data, and who will teach these groups?

3. Based on this information, write your team's SMART goal.

4. How does this goal support the building- or district-level goals?

5. As a collaborative team, choose instructional strategies that all members agree to use, and explain how they will be used in the classroom.

6. What data will be used in the PLC meetings to evaluate progress on the goal and your effectiveness in the classroom and as a team?

7. Describe how the collaborative team members will provide meaningful feedback to students about their performance to increase student learning.

8. Describe how the collaborative team members will provide meaningful feedback to families about their student's performance to increase student learning.

9. Describe how the collaborative team will use peer observation to provide feedback to teachers about the delivery of their lessons.

10. What training or support do you need from building or district staff to help achieve your objectives?

Source: Prompts written by Angie Peschel. Used with permission.

Figure A.2: Fall PLC goal-setting plan.

Use the following form (figure A.3) to guide PLC and evaluation process conversations between the principal or designee and the teacher. It was designed to have minimal written information but allow for rich conversations about the process. Such conversations are one of the desired outcomes of connecting PLC work and teacher evaluation.

Teacher: _____

School: _____

Principal or designee: _____

Date: _____

(If you answer "No" to any of these items, provide an explanation in the comments section.)

	Yes	No
PLC has used the Self-Evaluation Rubric to evaluate its effectiveness and to target areas of needed improvement.		
Teacher contributed to the PLC's effort to use data to set goal.		
PLC goal is SMART.		
The PLC goal supports building- and school-level goals.		
Teacher has identified what data will be used in PLC meetings to evaluate progress on the goal and effectiveness in the classroom.		
PLC has used the Plan-Do-Study-Act (PDSA) cycle to align its work and define next steps.		
PLC has defined how it will provide feedback to students.		
PLC has identified how it will provide meaningful feedback to families regarding their students' performance.		
PLC members have identified how they will use peer observation to provide feedback to each other.		
This teacher contributed to the PLC goal or plan and is committed to his or her individual responsibilities to the group effort.		

Comments

Additional information, training, or support needed:

Follow-up needed:

Follow-up strategies:

*Signature indicates discussion occurred but not that the teacher agrees with the comments in the form.

_____   _____
Teacher   Date   Administrator   Date

Teacher comments attached (optional).

Source: Mounds View Public Schools. Used with permission.

Figure A.3: Fall PLC conversation feedback form.

The following form (figure A.4) serves a similar purpose to the Fall PLC Conversation Feedback Form, allowing a rich midyear conversation about PLC work and the teacher evaluation process to occur between the principal or designee and the teacher.

Teacher: _____

School: _____

Principal or designee: _____

Date: _____

(If you answer "No" to any of the following, provide an explanation in the comments section.)

	Yes	No
PLC has used data to assess progress toward SMART goal.		
PLC has used PDSA cycle to identify next steps for individuals or groups of students who are not meeting achievement targets.		
PLC has identified how it will provide meaningful feedback to families of students not meeting achievement targets and identify appropriate interventions for them.		
PLC continues to use the Self-Evaluation Rubric to self-assess its efforts and identify where it needs to make changes to make progress on the rubric by the end of the year.		
Collaborative team has made growth on the effectiveness of the PLC.		
This individual teacher has contributed to the PLC process and has demonstrated growth on the effectiveness of the PLC.		

Figure A.4: Midyear PLC conversation feedback form.   Continued →

	Date	Date	Date
Walkthroughs			
PLC meeting observations			
Individual conversations			
Building leadership meetings			

Comments

Additional information, training, or support needed:

Follow-up needed:

Follow-up strategies:

*Signature indicates discussion occurred but not that the teacher agrees with the comments in the form.

_____   _____

Teacher   Date   Administrator   Date

Teacher comments attached (optional).

Source: Mounds View Public Schools. Used with permission.

The following form (figure A.5) serves a similar purpose to the fall and midyear forms, allowing a rich conversation about PLC work and the teacher evaluation process to occur between the principal or designee and the teacher at the end of the year.

Teacher: _____

School: _____

Principal or designee: _____

Date: _____

(If you answer "No" to any of the following, provide an explanation in the comments section.)

	Yes	No
Per the digital portfolio and observations, teacher attended all PLC meetings and contributed positively to the work of the PLC, for example, developing common assessments, review of data, identification of interventions, problem solving, and so on.		
Teacher employed methods and strategies identified by the PLC and the PDSA cycle in the classroom.		
Data from assessments indicates growth in achievement for all students and reflect progress toward the PLC goal and the Equity Promise.		
Parents received timely communication from this teacher regarding student progress.		
This individual teacher has worked with the PLC to use data to begin to identify implications for work in the next school year.		

	Date	Date	Date
Walkthroughs			
PLC meeting observations			
Individual conversations			
Building leadership meetings			
Formal and informal observations			

Comments

Areas of strength:

Areas of needed growth:

Follow-up strategies:

*Signature indicates discussion occurred but not that the teacher agrees with the comments in the form.

_____   _____
Teacher   Date   Administrator   Date

Teacher comments attached (optional).

Source: Mounds View Public Schools. Used with permission.

Figure A.5: End-of-year conversation feedback form.

The following form (figure A.6) provides specialized questions to guide conversations that are important for probationary staff to have with their principals.

Teacher: _____

School: _____

Principal or designee: _____

Date: _____

(If you answer "No" to any of the following, provide an explanation in the comments section.)

	Yes	No
Per the digital portfolio and observations, teacher attended all PLC meetings and contributed positively to the work of the PLC, for example, developing common assessments, review of data, identification of interventions, problem solving, and so on.		
Teacher employed methods and strategies identified by the PLC in the classroom.		
Data from assessments indicates growth in achievement for all students and reflects progress toward the PLC goals and the building goals.		
Parents received timely communication from this teacher regarding student progress.		
This individual teacher has worked with his or her PLC to use data to begin to identify implications for work in the next school year.		
This teacher has exhibited growth in the domains of:		
• Planning and preparation		
• Classroom environment		
• Instruction		
• Professional responsibility		

	Date	Date	Date
Walkthroughs			
PLC meeting observations			
Formal observations: post-observation meetings			

Comments

Areas of strength:

Areas of needed growth:

Follow-up strategies:

Building principal: check one of the following on final summary.

☐ Continue probationary status

☐ Place on continuing contract

☐ Termination

*Signature indicates discussion occurred but not that the teacher agrees with the comments in the form.

_____   _____

Teacher   Date   Administrator   Date

Teacher comments attached (optional).

Source: Mounds View Public Schools. Used with permission.

Figure A.6: Probationary staff end-of-year interactive feedback conversation form.

Conferencing Tools and Templates

The following tools and templates are designed to help you plan conferences with different types of teachers in a variety of situations throughout the supervision and evaluation process. Several templates include sample statements to guide you in developing your own script for a conference. Figure B.1 provides a tool to shape your conferences to address student achievement concerns with a teacher.

Use this template to guide your conversation with the teacher about the student achievement data concerns. Feel free to change this template or make adaptations to it based on your own unique needs or situation.

Set a Professional Tone

At the beginning of the conference, you'll want to set a professional tone. This will help keep the conversation on track. You may want to thank the teacher for meeting, share the importance of the conference, or make some other statement that lets the teacher know this is a crucial conversation and one that may be important to his or her future.

Provide an Overview of the Agenda for the Conference

By providing an overview of the conference agenda, you frame the conversation. This framing draws a boundary around the conversation to keep it focused during the conference.

Describe or Outline the Student Achievement Concern

It's important that you clearly identify the student achievement concern at this point in the conference. Be prepared to bring in specific data that reflect students are not performing according to expectations. Also, be ready to tie the student achievement concerns to areas of concern observed in the teaching. Connecting areas of concern will help you make the issues more clear and meaningful.

Figure B.1: Conferencing template for working with student achievement concerns.

Continued →

Give Clear, Clean Examples of the Deficiency and Why It Is a Deficiency

In this section of the conference, you need to provide the specific examples and evidence you have gathered that reflect the performance concerns. Providing evidence for student achievement scores should be fairly straightforward. Use the same precision when describing the related teaching performance concerns. By being clear and data driven in your descriptions, you help the teacher understand the issues.

Tell the Teacher He or She Is Not Meeting the Performance Standards

It might seem obvious, but it's important to tell the person that he or she is not meeting the standard or expectations. In these types of conferences, we want to be clear so there is no misunderstanding. By clearly stating that the teacher is not meeting the standards, you clearly define the issue.

Define the Required Skill or the Level of Performance Needed in Order to Meet the Standards

Now that you have told the teacher what is wrong, you need to let him or her know what you expect to happen in order for him or her to perform up to expectations. By defining this level of expectation, you help provide a target for the teacher to attain. Be clear by setting student-achievement benchmarks to guide the improvement process. You may need to establish periodic or ongoing performance goals to provide an opportunity for the teacher to improve.

Ask the Teacher to Share What He or She Learned in the Conference and What Changes Need to Occur in the Classroom

Now that you have clearly laid out the problem and the expectations, you need to make sure the teacher understands what was discussed in this conference. By taking the time to check the teacher's understanding, you eliminate the possibility of confusion and increase the level of accountability. Everyone should leave the conference with a clear understanding of the expectations and the next steps in the process.

Set Clear Expectations for Integration of the New Skill Into the Classroom, Including the Timeline for Implementation

The end of the conference is a good time to let the teacher know that you plan to follow up on the expectations set in this conference. One good way to do that is to tell the teacher that you plan to stop by to see how he is implementing the information discussed in the conference. Regarding student achievement data, you may want to follow up to include examination and discussion of periodic student achievement information from sources such as local assessments, unit tests, chapter tests, and so on to see whether the achievement issues are improving. Clearly communicating that you plan to follow up raises accountability but also lets the teacher know that you care and are willing to check in on his or her progress. This is a subtle but important message to communicate at the end of the conference.

Source: Adapted from Eller & Eller, 2010.

In order to say the crucial things in a conference while dealing with the feelings and emotions of the teacher you are conferencing with, develop a script to guide you through each conferencing experience. The sample statement starters in figure B.2 will assist you as you create scripts for your conferences.

You may find it helpful to use these statement starters for the more difficult conversations you may have with deficient teachers or in the termination process.

Statements Designed to Set a Professional Tone in a Difficult Conference

- "Thank you for meeting today to continue our discussions about your performance."
- "Thanks for taking the time to meet today."
- "I appreciate your professionalism as we talk about this difficult topic."
- "I know we come at this issue from different perspectives, but I appreciate your professionalism."
- "Thank you for meeting. I know this issue can be difficult to discuss."
- "As we continue to work together, we've had to discuss some difficult topics. Thank you for your professional attitude."
- "Even though I've shared my concerns with you in the past, it's important that we continue to meet and discuss your performance."

Statements Designed to Provide an Overview of the Agenda for the Conference

- "Today's conference will follow the same format as our previous conferences: I'll provide you with feedback about the most recent performance data I've gathered, I'll ask for your perceptions of these data, and I'll share how I think you're doing in relation to the performance expectations."
- "In our conference today, I will provide you with the feedback from my latest observation and let you know how I think you are doing with the improvement plan we are implementing."
- "In today's conference, I plan to give you an update on your progress and give you a chance to share your perspective, and then I'll share the next steps of the process."
- "In our meeting today, I need to provide you with an update on your progress. I know it's easy to get upset, but you need to think about what I've presented, and then we can talk after school about what you plan to do about the concerns."
- "The meeting today is focused on discussing your progress with your teaching. [Union rep's name], I know you're here as a representative from the union. Please listen until I finish presenting my performance information to [teacher's name]. After [teacher's name] and I complete our conference, I'll have [teacher's name] talk with you to see if you have any questions."
- "We both know the major issue here, so we'll start off the meeting with an update from you. I'll share the progress from my perspective, and then we'll decide if we want to refine the improvement plan we've designed."

Figure B.2: Sample statement starters for deficient teacher or termination conversations.

Continued →

Statements Designed to Address the Problem With the Teacher's Performance

- "In my most recent observations, I've continued to see areas of concern, such as _____. These teaching areas are still not meeting district standards."

- "I was in your classroom observing a lesson on _____. I still saw issues with _____. Your performance in this area is not meeting our standards."

- "I recently observed you as you've implemented _____. Your performance is better but still below our expectations. In order to meet the expectations, you'll need to _____."

- "In my most recent round of observations, I've seen you _____. You are slightly improving, but your overall performance is still below our district standards."

- "When I visited your classroom the other day, I saw you _____. As you know, this performance does not meet district standards for _____."

- "As you know, we have been focusing on _____ criteria during this school year. Your performance on this criteria area is below district standards."

- "Even though we have discussed my concerns about your classroom management, you still struggle in this area. Here are some examples from my most recent observation: _____. Your performance in this area is below the district's expectations. If I were to complete your summative evaluation at this point, I would have to rate you as not meeting district standards."

Statements Designed to Check the Person's Understanding of the Expectations for Performance

- "Before we conclude the meeting, let's review what we discussed and what you plan to address in your future lessons."

- "Please take a moment to summarize what we talked about today, what my expectations are regarding your teaching performance, and how you plan to continue to work on the areas of concern."

- "Even though this meeting was difficult, we were able to make some additional progress. Please take a few minutes to highlight the areas of growth and the continuing concerns. Also share your plans for working on _____."

- "It's my expectation that you will be able to continue to implement the major points that we talked about in our conference today. Please take a few minutes to outline those points and your plans to improve _____."

- "I know these conferences are not always easy for you, but I can see some progress in _____. Share what you learned in today's session and how you plan to continue to make changes."

- "Please tell me specifically what you took away from today's conference and how you plan to change your behavior."

- "We've talked about several topics today. What are the main points you are taking away from this conversation?"

- "If you were going to share the major points of our discussion with _____, what would they be?"

Follow-Up Statements Designed to Communicate Accountability for Teaching Performance

- "I have been clear in my continued expectations for your teaching performance. I plan to come to your classroom next week to see you."

- "You've made some progress, but we need to stay focused on _____. I'll stop by your class tomorrow to see how _____."

- "Since you understand what I need you to change, I expect to see these strategies employed in your classroom. I'll stop by sometime next week to see you use them and provide you with feedback."

- "You've been working to implement a plan for addressing your performance concerns. I'll stop by to _____."

- "I want to make sure that you have the support you need to _____. Let's continue to talk about this issue at our weekly meetings."

- "After you have had a chance to try the new ideas we discussed today, please set up a time to meet with me to fill me in on _____. Let's meet again in one week."

- "I'll contact [name of mentor] to work with you to set up classroom visitations for you. Let me know when your classroom visitation appointments are scheduled. I'd like to stop by while you are observing in a few of the classrooms. Once you have completed these visits, let's schedule a time to meet to talk about _____."

The following conferencing templates (figures B.3–B.6, pages 197–207) follow the same general structure of instructionally based supervision conferences as outlined in chapter 8 (page 119), but you will notice these templates contain some slight differences, depending on the specific situation or reason for the conference.

The template in figure B.3 is designed for conferences with marginal teachers who fit into the Challenged category. These conference components have been designed to fit together to provide a smooth conferencing experience. You can fill in your own words in the blank lines included in the sample statements.

Conferencing Phase I: Providing a Focus for the Conference

To best provide a focus for the conference, set the proper tone by letting the teacher know that the conference will be a professional experience. Sample statements include:

- "Thank you for coming in today to talk about your teaching. It's nice to have people like you who are dedicated to students working here. I know that

Figure B.3: Conferencing template for the Challenged. Continued →

your time is valuable, so I'll stay focused during this conference today."

- "Thank you for meeting with me today and talking about this professionally important topic."

- "Thanks for your willingness to get together and address this situation."

Next, provide an overview or outline for the conference. People like it when they know what to expect during a conference. Use this phase of the conference to lay out the plan for your time with the teacher. Sample statements include:

- "During this conference, I plan to ask you for your perception of the lesson; what you think went well and what you would change if you were to teach it again. Then I'll give you my perceptions of the effective areas and those that may need refinement. Finally, we'll explore how we can work together to continue to hone your teaching skills."

- "As we work together today to address the issue, we will use the following format:

  - "I'll share my concerns about _____."

  - "I'll give you a chance to respond to what I share with you about _____."

  - "Once both you and I are clear about the issue and how it came about, I'll have you share your strategies to address _____."

- "In this meeting, I'll share the details of the concern I briefly outlined when I was in your classroom and provide you with an opportunity to respond. Then we can develop a plan together."

Conferencing Phase II: Gaining Information and Feedback About the Teaching Performance

During the second phase, ask the teacher questions to help him or her reflect on the event and share his or her perceptions. It is important to find out what the teacher thought of the lesson. This helps build his or her reflective skills.

Be careful with this section because sometimes people think that the lesson was great when it was not. Don't just accept a teacher's perception if you have a different opinion about the lesson. Sample statements include:

- "As you think back to the lesson, how do you think things went overall? What went well? What didn't go as planned?"

- "From your perspective, what went well and what didn't go well in this lesson?"

- "As you think about your performance this year, talk about your areas of growth, and then share areas that continue to challenge you."

Next, the evaluator should provide specific feedback, including examples of effective teaching practices. In this section, you can give the teacher feedback about the lesson and what worked or went well from your perspective. Sample statements include:

- "As I watched the lesson, I noticed that _____ really seemed to be working well for you. That is an example of _____ from our teacher evaluation core competency list. Since it is effective, you should continue to use it in the future." (Up to three or four effective areas can be mentioned.)

- "In my observations, I've been able to see some positive trends in your teaching. Let me share a few of them here."

- "While there are many areas where you are doing a good job, three teaching areas stand out above the others. Let me share specific examples of when I've seen these used in your classroom, and the impact I observed on the students in your classes."

Then, tell the teacher what needs to be changed in his or her future teaching performance. This section of the conference is where you can thoroughly explain or teach something the teacher needs to improve or refine. Sample statements include:

- "One area that was not quite as effective as it could be was _____. Let me explain what this principle is all about. (Explains.) In the future, it is my expectation that you include this in your instruction to the students."

- "I've noticed in the last few walkthrough observations I've conducted that you have been _____. This behavior is still a little below the district standards."

- "In examining your assessment data, I found that _____. This indicates to me that students are making very little growth in the areas of _____."

Conferencing Phase III: Ensuring the Major Recommendations From the Conference Are Applied in the Classroom

In the third phase, begin by asking questions to make sure the teacher understands the marginal area and what his or her expectations are for the needed improvement. Making sure the teacher understands the issue and what improvement you expect is key to your success as an administrator. Asking clear questions to ensure that the teacher understands can feel unnatural, but it ensures that your expectations are clear. Now, if the performance does not improve, you can move forward in taking additional actions because you are sure the teacher understood what needed to be changed. Sample questions include:

- "I want to make sure you are successful in changing _____. What are my expectations, and when do I want you to be implementing them?"

- "If you were going to share the major points of our discussion with _____, what would they be?"

- "This conversation was very productive and important to your future here at _____. What is your understanding of my expectations for your behavior?"

- "Before we leave today, let's take a minute to review what was discussed and what we agreed on as a result of our time together today."

Finally, share the plan for follow-up to ensure the recommended changes are made in the classroom. Follow-up is essential to the success of any teacher evaluation process. Here you plan to check in with the teacher in the future to make sure that the refinement area you shared is being implemented. Sample statements include:

- "We both agree that _____ is an important area for you to use in your teaching. I'll stop back in a couple of weeks to see how you are integrating it into your teaching."

Continued →

- "Now that we both are on the same page, I plan to come to your classroom next week to see you _____."
- "In order to support you through this change, I plan to stop by next week to talk with you about how you have _____."
- "As you develop _____, you need to send them to me so I can review them before _____."

The template in figure B.4 is designed for conferences with marginal teachers who fit into the On-the-Job Retiree category. These conference components have been designed to fit together to provide a smooth conferencing experience. You can fill in your own words in the blank lines included in the sample statements.

Conferencing Phase I: Providing a Focus for the Conference

To best provide a focus for the conference, set the proper tone by letting the teacher know that the conference will be a professional experience. Sample statements include:

- "I appreciate the time you set aside to meet with me. I know you have been effective in the past and want to return to your high level of effectiveness."
- "I appreciate you taking the time to meet with me today to clear up this issue."
- "Thank you for your focus on this issue and for meeting with me to clarify it."
- "I know it's not always easy to talk about these types of situations, but I do appreciate that you are willing to work with me to get to the bottom of this issue."

Next, provide an overview or outline for the conference. People like it when they know what to expect during a conference. Use this phase of the conference to lay out the plan for your time with the teacher. Sample statements include:

- "Today, I'd like to spend some time talking about your teaching, what is working, and areas of challenge for you. I'd like to get your ideas about how you'd like to improve. Then we can talk about a plan to move forward."
- "We both know the major issue here, so we'll start off the meeting with an update from you. I'll share the progress from my perspective, and then we'll decide the next steps in the process."
- "During this meeting, I need to share a concern I have with your performance. I'll give you a chance to share your side of the story, and then I'll take your thoughts into consideration to develop a plan to stop the problem behavior."
- "In our meeting today, I want to share my concerns, give you a chance to think about them, and get together later to _____."

Conferencing Phase II: Gaining Information and Feedback About the Teaching Performance

During the second phase, ask the teacher questions to help him or her reflect on the event and share his or her perceptions. It is important to find out what the teacher thought of the lesson. This helps build his or her reflective skills.

Be careful with this section because sometimes people think that the lesson was great when it was not. Don't just accept a teacher's perception if you have a different opinion about the lesson. Sample statements include:

- "Let's have an open conversation about the areas of challenge you face in your teaching. What do you notice when _____?"

- "How does what actually happened in the lesson match your plan? What is different from what you had planned?"

- "What went as you expected? What surprises did you experience in the lesson?"

- "What do you think went well, and what challenges did you face in this lesson?"

Next, provide specific feedback including examples of effective teaching practices. In this section, you can give the teacher feedback about the lesson and what worked or went well from your perspective. Sample statements include:

- "As I have watched you teach in your classroom this year, there are several areas where you are doing well. They are _____."

- "In my observations over the course of the year, I have noticed there are some areas that are consistently working for you."

- "There are several areas where you are on track with the district's expectations. Let me focus on two of those areas here."

Then, tell the teacher what needs to be changed in his or her future teaching performance. This section of the conference is where you can thoroughly explain or teach something the teacher needs to improve or refine. Sample statements include:

- "In my assessment of your teaching, I observed that you are struggling with _____. Here are some of the examples I have observed over the last few months."

- "In my observations, I've noticed that you are _____. This is not in compliance with our standards, and it needs to be addressed immediately."

- "When watching you interact in staff meetings, I've noticed that you _____. This behavior is diminishing your professional position with the staff. You need to _____."

- "In talking with _____, it has come to my attention that _____. This behavior needs to stop immediately and _____."

- "On Tuesday, I saw you _____. You know this behavior is outside the boundaries of my expectations and needs to be addressed immediately."

Figure B.4: Conferencing template for On-the-Job Retirees.

Continued →

Conferencing Phase III: Ensuring the Major Recommendations From the Conference Are Applied in the Classroom

In the third phase, begin by asking questions to make sure the teacher understands the marginal area and what his or her expectations are for the needed improvement. Making sure the teacher understands the issue and what improvement you expect is key to your success as an administrator. Asking clear questions to ensure that the teacher understands can feel unnatural, but it ensures that your expectations are clear. Now, if the performance does not improve, you can move forward in taking additional actions because you are sure the teacher understood what needed to be changed. Sample questions include:

- "What, specifically, will you take away from today's conference, and how do you plan to change your behavior?"

- "How would you summarize what we talked about today, what my expectations are in relation to this type of behavior, and what you need to do to address these expectations?"

- "We've talked about several topics today. What are the main points you are taking away from this conversation?"

Finally, share the plan for follow-up to ensure the recommended changes are made in the classroom. Follow-up is essential to the success of any teacher evaluation process. Here you plan to check in with the teacher in the future to make sure that the refinement area you shared is being implemented. Sample statements include:

- "I know that you are interested in working to get back to the high levels of teaching you were at in the past. I am willing to do the following to help you _____."

- "I want to make sure that you have the support you need to _____. Let's meet to talk about this issue on a monthly basis."

- "After you have had a chance to _____, set up a time to fill me in on _____. Let's say that we'll meet again in two weeks."

The template in figure B.5 is designed for conferences with marginal teachers who fit into the Resident Expert category. These conference components have been designed to fit together to provide a smooth conferencing experience. You can fill in your own words in the blank lines included in the sample statements.

Conferencing Phase I: Providing a Focus for the Conference

To best provide a focus for the conference, set the proper tone by letting the teacher know that the conference will be a professional experience. Sample statements include:

- "I appreciate you taking the time to meet with me today. In this conference, we will focus on improving your teaching skills."

- "I know we have not always agreed on issues in the past, but thank you for meeting with me today to come to some common ground on this situation."

- "Even though we come from different perspectives on this situation, we can work together to design a plan to address the issue and move forward."

Next, provide an overview or outline for the conference. People like it when they know what to expect during a conference. Use this phase of the conference to lay out the plan for your time with the teacher. Sample statements include:

- "In this conference, I will provide you with feedback about your teaching and the areas where need you to improve."

- "In today's conference, I plan to give you an update on your progress, give you a chance to clear up anything I've told you, and then I'll share the next steps of the plan I've developed for _____."

- "In our meeting today, I need to make you aware of some concerns I've heard about _____. I don't need you to respond to them yet, but just listen to them. After the meeting, I'll ask you to go back and think about what I've shared with you in relation to _____. Then be ready to meet with me in a few days to share your perspective and develop a plan to _____."

- "In our time together today, I want to address _____, which I need you to stop doing immediately."

- "In our conference today, I'll share my concerns about your situation, and then you can share your perspective on it. Finally, we'll develop a plan to address _____."

Conferencing Phase II: Gaining Information and Feedback About the Teaching Performance

During the second phase, provide specific feedback including examples of effective teaching practices. When working with Resident Experts, be careful not to provide too much feedback about effective teaching practices. Resident Experts can take one or two statements and overgeneralize. At times, they may also use your compliments against you. You will want to provide positive feedback, but be sure to moderate it in your conferences. Sample statements include:

- "In my observations, I noted that you are doing a good job in the area of _____."

- "Even though we have concentrated on the areas where you need improvement, I want you to know there some areas where you are meeting the standard in your teaching."

- "Let me share an area where your teaching is on track. We may want to use this strength to help overcome the areas of concern I have expressed regarding your performance."

- "As we continue to work together, I'd like to give you some feedback about where you have shown some improvement. These areas still need work, but I see you are moving in the right direction."

Then, tell the teacher what needs to be changed in his or her future teaching performance. This section of the conference is where you can thoroughly explain or teach something the teacher needs to improve or refine. Sample statements include:

Figure B.5: Conferencing template for Resident Experts. Continued →

- "Last Wednesday in your classroom, I saw you _____. This kind of behavior is not meeting our standards for teachers. You need to address this behavior and correct it immediately."

- "I've noticed in the last few walkthrough observations that I've conducted that you have been _____.This behavior is not meeting district standards."

- "When I visited your classroom the other day, I saw you _____. As you know, this performance does not meet district standards for _____."

- "When I compare your _____ with the rest of the building, I see that your students are not making the kind of progress that others are making. This shows me that you are not meeting standards on criteria _____."

- "As you know, we have been focusing on criteria _____ during this school year. Your performance on this criteria area is below district standards."

- "In my informal observations this fall, I noticed that you _____. I have talked with you about this problem in the past, but you continue to teach in this manner. Your performance in this area is not meeting district standards at this time."

- "You continue to have difficulty _____. I have noticed a lack of _____ in my formal and informal observations and have shared my concerns with you. At this point in the year, you are not meeting district standards in the area of _____."

- "Even though we have discussed my concerns regarding _____, you still struggle in this area. Here are some recent examples where you have not _____. Your performance is below the district's expectations in this area. If I were to complete your summative evaluation at this point, I would have to rate you as not meeting district standards."

Conferencing Phase III: Ensuring the Major Recommendations From the Conference Are Applied in the Classroom

In the third phase, begin by making sure the teacher understands the marginal area and what his or her expectations are for the needed improvement. Making sure the teacher understands the issue and what improvement you expect is key to your success as an administrator. Asking clear questions to ensure that the teacher understands can feel unnatural, but it ensures that your expectations are clear. Now, if the performance does not improve, you can move forward in taking additional actions because you are sure the teacher understood what needed to be changed. Sample prompts include:

- "Even though this meeting was difficult, we were able to accomplish several key points today. Please take a few minutes to highlight those and your plans for addressing _____."

- "It's my expectation that you will be able to implement the major points that we talked about in our conference today. Please take a few minutes to outline those points and your plans to improve _____."

- "I know these conferences are not always easy for you, but I can see some progress in _____. Help me understand what you got out of today's session and what will change as a result."

Finally, share the plan for follow-up to ensure the recommended changes are made in the classroom. Follow-up is essential to the success of any teacher evaluation process. Here you plan to check in with the teacher in the future to make sure that the refinement area you shared is being implemented. Sample statements include:

- "I want to make sure that you improve your teaching in this area. I plan to stop by to watch as you implement _____."
- "Since you understand what I need you to change, I expect to see _____ in your future lesson plans. I'll be reviewing them and giving you feedback."
- "Since we now have a plan in place for addressing concerns, I expect you to set up an appointment with me in the future when we _____."

The conferencing template in figure B.6 is designed specifically for conversations regarding summative evaluations.

Conferencing Phase I: Providing a Focus for the Conference

To best provide a focus for the conference, set the proper tone by letting the teacher know that the conference will be a professional experience. Sample statements include:

- "I appreciate you taking the time to meet today to discuss your overall performance for the school year."
- "Thank you for meeting with me today to discuss your summative evaluation."
- "Thanks for meeting today. I appreciate how seriously you take your professional growth."

Next, provide an overview or outline for the conference. People like it when they know what to expect during a conference. Use this phase of the conference to lay out the plan for your time with the teacher. Sample statements include:

- "During this conference, I'd like to share some of my thoughts about your performance this school year. I'd then like to hear some of your thoughts or feedback about how you feel you've done. Then we'll talk about how we can use both perspectives to develop your summative evaluation document."
- "In today's summative conference, I'll share the overall strengths I saw when looking at multiple data sources related to your performance. Then we'll work together to develop your professional growth plan for the next school year."
- "Today, we are here to discuss your summative evaluation conference. I'll ask you to sum up your thoughts and perspectives for the year, and then I'll share my feedback on your overall performance. Finally, we'll look at strategies for the next school year."

Conferencing Phase II: Gaining Information and Feedback About the Teaching Performance

During the second phase, ask the teacher questions to help him or her reflect on his or her performance for the year. Also ask the teacher to share the data used to develop his or her conclusions (used for all summative conferences). It is important to gather the teacher's perceptions of his or her performance during the year and the evidence

---

Figure B.6: Conferencing template for summative evaluations.

Continued →

or data he or she used to develop these perceptions. Be sure to ask the teacher to share the data he or she used to develop this conclusion and tell you how these data relate to his or her performance. Don't just accept a teacher's perception if you have a different opinion about his or her performance. Sample statements include:

- "As you think back on your year, how do you think things went overall? What went well? What didn't go as planned?"
- "From your perspective, what are some of your strengths as a teacher? What are some of your limitations or areas where you could continue to grow as a teacher?"
- "As you think about your performance this year, talk about your areas of growth, and then share areas that continue to challenge you."

Next, provide specific feedback including examples of effective teaching practices. Share your positive rating or score within each area. Share the evidence or rationale you used to develop that rating. Ask the teacher for his or her perspective.

During this part of the conference, provide the teacher with his or her effective performance ratings and the evidence you used to develop these ratings. In many cases, you may not have comprehensive data to document each score, so you'll want to involve the teacher in the discussion of the effective measures. You may decide to adjust your ratings as a result of the teacher's feedback or perspective of his or her overall performance. Sample statements include:

- "I have had a chance to review all of the data related to your teaching performance this year. Let me share your areas of strength and how I rated your overall performance. The strongest area for you is _____. In this area, I have found _____. Your efforts in this area are well above the expectations of the building; therefore I'm rating you as _____."
- "In my observations, I've been able to see some positive trends in your teaching. Let me share a few of them here and how they impacted your overall summative evaluation rating."
- "While there are many areas where you are doing a good job, three teaching areas stand out above the others. Let me share specific examples, of when I've seen these used in your classroom, and the impact I observed on the students in your classes."

Next, present information about growth needs or areas that need to be changed in the future. Share the summative scores for these areas and the data or rationale used to develop these scores. Let the teacher share his or her perspective on the areas for growth and the summative scores.

In this part of the conference, discuss or explain any areas in the summative report where the teacher has scores that indicate growth is needed. You'll want to get the teacher's perspective on these areas so you can determine if there are data you missed in determining the teacher's summative performance score. You'll also want to let the teacher share any background information that might help explain any apparent deficits in the area. Some of the information you gain from the teacher may justify adjusting his or her summative score, may help you establish a focus for the upcoming year, or may require the teacher to be more involved in gathering data for documentation. In any case, you'll want to be open to listening to the feedback of the teacher while also being aware that you may need to stand firm on your summative score even if you and the teacher have different perspectives. As the evaluator, you are the authority who determines the final performance evaluation score. Sample statements include:

- "In your overall teaching performance, one area that was not quite as effective as it could be was _____. I rated the area as needs continued emphasis. I'll share the data I used to rate this area and then let you share some of the data you have for this area."

- "As a result of the walkthroughs I've conducted this year and our work together in examining your curriculum units, I notice the area of content knowledge is still an area where you need to continue to grow. Let's talk about this area, your summative score, and plans to continue to address this area in the future."

Conferencing Phase III: Ensuring the Major Recommendations From the Conference and the Summative Evaluation Are Applied in the Classroom

In the third phase, begin by asking questions to make sure the teacher understands both the strengths and the growth areas related to his or her performance and the expectations for the next evaluation cycle. Understanding the teacher's strengths and areas of needed refinement are key to the evaluation process. If you are working to measure the teaching performance (evaluation), you'll want to ensure that the teacher understands the scope of his or her performance. If you are working to help your teachers grow (supervision), you'll want to make sure the teacher understands the needed areas of growth and the strengths he or she possesses that may assist in his or her growth. Example questions include:

- "I want to make sure you are successful in changing _____. What are the areas we talked about today that are strengths for you? What are the areas we talked about where you need to grow? How can you use your strengths to help work with your areas for growth?"

- "If you were going to share the major points of our discussion with _____, what would they be?"

- "This conversation was very productive and important to your future here at _____. What's your understanding of my expectations for your teaching?"

- "Before we leave today, let's take a minute to review what was discussed and what we agreed on as a result of our time together."

Finally, share the plan for follow-up to ensure that the recommended changes are made in the classroom. Follow-up is essential to the success of any teacher evaluation process. In this section of the conference, you'll develop strategies to work with the teacher to maintain his or her existing skill set and to make the needed changes to help him or her grow as a teacher. Sample statements include:

- "We both agree that _____ is an important area for you to use in your teaching. How do you plan to continue to grow in this area?"

- "Now that we both are on the same page about your teaching, let's talk about how we can integrate this aspect into your next professional growth goal."

- "In order to support you through this change, it would be good for you to think about how you can use the peer review part of our evaluation plan to _____."

- "You are scheduled to be in the informal evaluation phase next year. I want to continue to formally observe you in the area of _____ so we can work together to help you keep growing. Let's talk about _____."

*Visit **go.solution-tree.com/leadership** for a reproducible version of this figure.*

References and Resources

Abrams, J. (2009). *Having hard conversations*. Thousand Oaks, CA: Corwin Press.

Aseltine, J. M., Faryniarz, J. O., & Rigazio-DiGilio, A. J. (2006). *Supervision for learning: A performance-based approach to teacher development and school improvement*. Alexandria, VA: Association for Supervision and Curriculum Development.

Cantrell, S., & Kane, T. J. (2013). *Ensuring fair and reliable measures of effective teaching: Culminating findings from the MET project's three-year study*. Accessed at http://metproject.org/downloads/MET_Ensuring_Fair_and _Reliable_Measures_Practitioner_Brief.pdf on September 15, 2014.

Carey, W. C. (1988). *Documenting teacher dismissal: A guide for the site administrator* (2nd ed.). Salem, OR: Options Press.

Costa, A. L., & Garmston, R. J. (2002). *Cognitive coaching: A foundation for renaissance schools* (2nd ed.). Norwood, MA: Christopher-Gordon.

Danielson, C., & McGreal, T. L. (2000). *Teacher evaluation to enhance professional practice*. Alexandria, VA: Association for Supervision and Curriculum Development.

Danielson Group. (2013). *Danielson rubrics*. (n.d.). Accessed at www.danielsongroup .org/article.aspx?page=frameworkforteaching on October 16, 2014.

DeMitchell, T. A. (1995). Competence, documentation, and dismissal: A legal template. *International Journal of Educational Reform, 4*(1), 88–95.

DuFour, R., DuFour, R., Eaker, R., & Many, T. W. (2010). *Learning by doing: A handbook for professional learning communities at work* (2nd ed.). Bloomington, IN: Solution Tree Press.

DuFour, R., & Marzano, R. J. (2011). *Leaders of learning: How district, school, and classroom leaders improve student achievement*. Bloomington, IN: Solution Tree Press.

Elgin, S. H. (1985). *The gentle art of verbal self-defense.* Englewood Cliffs, NJ: Prentice Hall.

Eller, J. (2004). *Effective group facilitation in education: How to energize meetings and manage difficult groups.* Thousand Oaks, CA: Corwin Press.

Eller, J., & Carlson, H. C. (2009). *So now you're the superintendent!* Thousand Oaks, CA: Corwin Press.

Eller, J. F., & Eller, S. (2009). *Creative strategies to transform school culture.* Thousand Oaks, CA: Corwin Press.

Eller, J. F., & Eller, S. (2010). *Working with and evaluating difficult school employees.* Thousand Oaks, CA: Corwin Press.

Eller, J. F., & Eller, S. (2011). *Working with difficult and resistant staff.* Bloomington, IN: Solution Tree Press.

Eller, S., & Eller, J. (2006). *Energizing staff meetings.* Thousand Oaks, CA: Corwin Press.

Garrett, K. (2011). Value added: Do new teacher evaluation methods make the grade? *Education Digest: Essential Readings Condensed for Quick Review, 77*(2), 40–45.

Glatthorn, A. A. (1997). *Differentiated supervision* (2nd ed.). Alexandria, VA: Association for Supervision and Curriculum Development.

Glickman, C. D. (2002). *Leadership for learning: How to help teachers succeed.* Alexandria, VA: Association for Supervision and Curriculum Development.

Goldstein, J. (2005). Debunking the fear of peer review: Combining supervision and evaluation and living to tell about it. *Journal of Personnel Evaluation in Education, 18*(4), 235–252.

Goleman, D., Boyatzis, R., & McKee, A. (2002). *Primal leadership: Realizing the power of emotional intelligence.* Cambridge, MA: Harvard Business School Press.

Hattie, J. (2009). *Visible learning: A synthesis of over 800 meta-analyses relating to achievement.* New York: Routledge.

Hattie, J. (2012). *Visible learning for teachers: Maximizing impact on learning.* New York: Routledge.

Johnson, S. M., & Fiarman, S. E. (2012). The potential of peer review. *Educational Leadership, 70*(3), 20–25.

Kanold, T. D. (2011). *The five disciplines of PLC leaders.* Bloomington, IN: Solution Tree Press.

Kaye, E. B. (2004). Turning the tide on marginal teaching. *Journal of Curriculum and Supervision, 19*(3), 234–258.

Kochanek, J. R. (2005). *Building trust for better schools: Research-based practices.* Thousand Oaks, CA: Corwin Press.

Kuhn, T. S. (1996). *The structure of scientific revolutions* (3rd ed.). Chicago: University of Chicago Press.

Lawrence, C. E. (2005). *The marginal teacher: A step-by-step guide to fair procedures for identification and dismissal* (3rd ed.). Thousand Oaks, CA: Corwin Press.

Leo, S., & Lachlan-Haché, L. (2012). *Creating summative educator effectiveness scores: Approaches to combining measures.* Washington, DC: American Institutes for Research.

Lipton, L., & Wellman, B. (2003). *Mentoring matters: A practical guide to learning-focused relationships* (2nd ed.). Sherman, CT: MiraVia.

Marshall, K. (2012). Fine-tuning teacher evaluation. *Educational Leadership, 70*(3), 50–53.

Marshall, K. (2014). Teacher evaluation rubrics. Accessed at http://www.marshallmemo .com/articles/%20Teacher%20rubrics%20Jan%202014%20corr.pdf on February 2, 2015.

Marzano, R. J. (2003). *Classroom management that works: Research-based strategies for every teacher.* Alexandria, VA: Association for Supervision and Curriculum Development.

Marzano, R. J. (2007). *The art and science of teaching: A comprehensive framework for effective instruction.* Alexandria, VA: Association for Supervision and Curriculum Development.

Marzano, R. J., Frontier, T., & Livingston, D. (2011). *Effective supervision: Supporting the art and science of teaching.* Alexandria, VA: Association for Supervision and Curriculum Development.

Marzano, R. J., & Toth, M. D. (2013). *Teacher evaluation that makes a difference: A new model for teacher growth and student achievement.* Alexandria, VA: Association for Supervision and Curriculum Development.

McLaughlin, M., Vogt, M. E., Anderson, J., DuMez, J., Peter, M. G., & Hunter, A. (1998). *Professional portfolio models: Applications in education.* Norwood, MA: Christopher-Gordon.

Milanowski, A. (2011). Strategic measures of teacher performance. *Phi Delta Kappan, 92*(7), 19–25.

My Student Survey. (n.d.). *2010–11 student survey results.* Accessed at http:// mystudentsurvey.com/wp-content/uploads/2011/11/Teacher-Report-Sample -Final-2.pdf on April 22, 2014.

My Student Survey. (2014). *Student survey teacher report.* Accessed at http:// mystudentsurvey.com/reports/sample on February 2, 2015.

National Council on Teacher Quality. (2012). *State of the states 2012: Teacher effectiveness policies.* Accessed at www.nctq.org/dmsView/State_of_the _States_2012_Teacher_Effectiveness_Policies_NCTQ_Report on April 22, 2014.

National Governors Association Center for Best Practices & Council of Chief State School Officers. (2010). *Common Core State Standards.* Washington, DC: Authors.

Pollock, J. E., & Ford, S. M. (2009). *Improving student learning one principal at a time.* Alexandria, VA: Association for Supervision and Curriculum Development.

Sagor, R. (2011). *The action research guidebook: A four-stage process for educators and school teams* (2nd ed.). Thousand Oaks, CA: Corwin Press.

Schein, E. H. (2010). *Organizational culture and leadership* (4th ed.). San Francisco: Jossey-Bass.

Stronge, J. H. (2015). *Stronge teacher evaluation system.* Accessed at www.njea.org /news-and-publications/njea-review/november-2011/comparing-teacher -evaluation-models/stronge on February 2, 2015.

Toch, T. (2008). Fixing teacher evaluation. *Educational Leadership, 66*(2), 32–37.

Washington State Teacher/Principal Evaluation Project. (2013). *The Marzano teacher evaluation model at a glance.* Accessed at http://tpep-wa.org /wp-content/uploads/Marzano-at-a-glance.pdf on April 22, 2014.

Wheatley, M. J. (1992). *Leadership and the new science: Learning about organization from an orderly universe.* San Francisco: Berrett-Koehler.

Index

Working With Difficult & Resistant Staff
John F. Eller, Sheila A. Eller
Identify, confront, and manage all of the difficult and resistant staff you encounter. This book will help school leaders understand how to prevent and address negative staff behaviors to ensure positive school change.
BKF407

How to Interview, Hire, & Retain High-Quality New Teachers (Third Edition)
John C. Daresh, Bridget N. Daresh
The key to student success starts in the classroom. The authors use firsthand experiences and observations to guide readers through effective processes for recruiting, interviewing, hiring, and supporting faculty who best fit the needs of individual schools.
BKF447

Learning by Doing (Second Edition)
Richard DuFour, Rebecca DuFour, Robert Eaker, and Thomas W. Many
This book is an action guide for closing the knowing-doing gap and transforming schools into PLCs. It includes seven major additions that equip educators with essential tools for confronting challenges.
BKF416

Leading Difficult Conversations [DVD/CD/Facilitator's Guide]
Richard DuFour, Rebecca DuFour
Gain strategies for addressing the conflicts that can result from transforming a school into a professional learning community. Learn how to hold conversations that lead staff to understand that best practice is to work collaboratively and collectively in high-performing teams.
DVF047

Solution Tree | Press
a division of
Solution Tree

Visit solution-tree.com or call 800.733.6786 to order.

Wait! Your professional development journey doesn't have to end with the last pages of this book.

We realize improving student learning doesn't happen overnight. And your school or district shouldn't be left to puzzle out all the details of this process alone.

No matter where you are on the journey, we're committed to helping you get to the next stage.

Take advantage of everything from **custom workshops** to **keynote presentations** and **interactive web and video conferencing**. We can even help you develop an action plan tailored to fit your specific needs.

Let's get the conversation started.

Call 888.763.9045 today.

solution-tree.com